EMBODYING MARK

*Fresh ways to read,
pray and live the Gospel*

Meda A. A. Stamper

*Wishing you well
on your journey
with the Beloved,*

Meda

SPCK

First published in Great Britain in 2014

Society for Promoting Christian Knowledge
36 Causton Street
London SW1P 4ST
www.spckpublishing.co.uk

British Library Cataloguing-in-Publication Data
A catalogue record for this book is available from the British Library

ISBN 978–0–281–07261–3
eBook ISBN 978–0–281–07262–0

Typeset by Graphicraft Limited, Hong Kong
First printed in Great Britain by Ashford Colour Press
Subsequently digitally printed in Great Britain

eBook by Graphicraft Limited, Hong Kong

Produced on paper from sustainable forests

Contents

Words of thanks

I have come to regard this little book as a love letter to God and to my neighbours on the way of the Beloved. I am grateful to SPCK for giving me this opportunity, and I am grateful to the people who nurture in me the kind of love I talk about here and who make good things possible through their presence in my life. Among those beautiful friends, a few have shown me particular kindness in the course of this project. Thank you to Andy, Becky, Beth, CC, Charlie, Elizabeth, John, Kirk, Sally and Sara (and others I will remember as soon as it is too late to add them here) for their encouragement, help and prayers; to my gentle family of faith at Anstey URC for listening lovingly as I preached my way through things; to Aunt Sally, who deserves a small book of thanks of her own for proofreading the book multiple times, creating the index, and being constantly joyful about all of it; and to Robert for walking with me through the muddy and the golden and loving me all along the way.

Introduction

You are invited on an eight-stage journey with Jesus, God's Beloved, through the Gospel of Mark.

This is your guidebook to a multi-dimensional experience of this story. You will be invited to explore Mark creatively, intellectually, spiritually, physically and emotionally, and to discover in your exploration of the story an encounter with God, who loves you and who sends you out to embody that divine 'I love you' in the world in a way that only you can.

You can take this holy journey on your own or with a group. You can spend as little or as much time as is possible and desirable for you. Just as an afternoon in Paris would be worthwhile and a year even better, so any length of time exploring Mark will be well spent. You could dedicate a long weekend to reading this whole book and all of Mark on your own. Or you could have a series of weekly, biweekly or monthly meetings or mini-retreats with a group (see 'Suggestions for groups' below).

Because Mark is endlessly fascinating and infinitely rich, the experience offered by this book can be repeated at different times in your life, and each experience will reveal something new about God, the Gospel and you.

Whenever you are ready, you have an open invitation to set out on your adventure with the Beloved – and to see what happens next.

How to use this book

Each chapter is orientated around a **Focus text**. Alongside each of these is a longer **Reading through Mark**, which places the text in context and also guides you through the whole of the Gospel by the end of this book. Each chapter has a theme, drawn from the text and reflected in the chapter title. Most of these invite you to consider something about

Jesus as you follow him through the Gospel. The first and last depart from this slightly in ways that will make sense as you read them.

Read each text aloud, or hear it read in a group or with a friend. The Gospel was written at a time when few people could read. Stories circulated orally. Then, once they were written down, one person would read them aloud to others. Even on their own, people probably did not read silently (Acts 8.30). When you experience the text aloud, you are doing what it expects you to do. Try reading in the voice you would use if you were telling a story to a friend, with that kind of enthusiasm, pleasure and emotion. If you are reading for others, consider yourself the bearer of God's good news, a gift of love, because that is what you are (Isaiah 52.7).

As part of your exploration of each text, try praying it.

Praying the text

This process is flexible, beautiful and fruitful. You will find that you can do this in whatever time is available to you and in any setting. It can take two minutes or as long as you want it to take; if you wish, you can carry a word, image or phrase with you and leave the door of your mind open to God all day. Once you have experienced this once or twice, you will not need to refer to these instructions again, but feel free to return to any parts that could help you as you pray (or as you lead others in prayer); sometimes having someone else with us in prayer, even only in writing, can be good. This practice is also called *lectio divina*; search online for that phrase if you'd like to know more.

1 Become physically present

Sit comfortably upright with your legs uncrossed and both feet on the ground (you may stand, lie or walk if sitting is uncomfortable for you or if you happen to be walking, standing or lying when you want to do this). Lift your shoulders and place them back gently on your torso. Adjust your abdomen if you need to by pulling it back slightly so that you are straight and not swaybacked. Imagine a cord pulling up gently through the crown of your head so that your head sits lightly on your neck. Rest your hands comfortably on your lap. If you are holding tension anywhere (shoulders, face, hands), let that tension gently fall away. Close your eyes if you wish. Notice how your body feels, your feet against the floor, your weight against the chair. Notice the temperature in the room, whether the air is moving or still. Attend to the feel of the air in your nostrils and in your lungs.

2 Become mentally present

Direct your attention to this moment in your life as you prepare to meet God in the text. Become aware of what you hear around you, what you smell and (if your eyes are open) what you see. Observe what is going through your mind; then let it drift by as you let the tension drift from your body. Give yourself permission to lay aside temporarily anything that is drawing your attention away from the present, with the assurance that you can think about that again later. If it helps to set a time limit, then assure yourself you will pick back up where you left off in precisely that time. If it helps to make notes of things that are pressing on you in order to lay those aside, do that. If it helps to place some concern or question in the hands of God or to place your entire self before God in your mind's eye, do so. Then continue gently and kindly redirecting your thoughts and energy to the present moment (relaxing your face and shoulders again, as needed).

3 Become present to God, and become aware of God present with you in love

You might imagine opening the door of your mind to God, or you might imagine walking towards God. You will find that as you sit in silent expectation, images of God will come to you. These may be different at different times. Some may stick with you for ever; others may be fleeting. Allow yourself to engage with these different images and draw near to ones that are most loving to you. For some of us, the image of God as a father is extremely comforting. For others, a female image for God can be healing. Male and female human beings are both created in God's image; both can show us things about God's love, and yet God is beyond either of those. The key thing is that God loves you, so you may open your imagination to images of love and see what the Spirit offers. You may find yourself drawn to an image of Jesus in his humanity. You may be drawn to an image of the Spirit – in fire, cloud, darkness, light, the sound of the wind, the descent of a dove. You may find that an image of the Creator–Father–Mother–Lion–Dew–Lover–Warrior–Shepherd (all images for God in Scripture) first member of the Trinity draws you. Approach whatever image best directs you to the Beautiful Mystery of the one who loves you now in this moment precisely as you are today.

4 Read the text slowly with God

Feel free to pause over any word, image or theme that draws you. Dwell in the moment in the text with whatever thoughts, questions or feelings it raises. You need not read to the end. Bring yourself to the text in the presence of God in the way that you might sit with a person you love over a hot drink or an iced tea and share a story or a word of encouragement. The words might be important to both of you and might tell you something about your friend or yourself, and you might remember them for ever; but the most important thing in that moment (the thing that makes the words possible) is the love you share with your friend.

5 Speak to God

When you have read all of the text (or as much as you wish), commune with God in your mind's eye or aloud. Is there a particular image, phrase or theme you'd like to lay before God as a gift or a question? Has the text raised any feelings or memories you'd like to share? The text may evoke something that seems utterly unrelated to it, and that may be the gift that it gives you today and the prayer that it opens up. If nothing comes to you, that is also perfectly fine. Being present with God in the moment is all that matters.

6 Sit in silence

When you have finished, sit with God. You may think of this as listening for God. You may think of it as being still and knowing that God is God (Psalm 46.10), which is sometimes what we most need. God is always happy to have you there, and spending time in the presence of divine love makes us blossom.

The **Thinking about** section offers food for thought about the 'Focus text' and the theme for each chapter. You are invited to explore the Gospel as a story and to consider how you might locate yourself in that story. The Gospels each tell God's love story with the world, and if we choose to follow Jesus, we become living embodiments of that love. The 'Thinking about' sections give you a chance to ponder how Mark's particular telling speaks to you.

Alongside attention to the details of the text, these sections also explore the larger context of Mark. Individual passages often become richer and clearer when we see how they fit into the full sweep of the narrative. The study also draws connections to other parts of Scripture and situates the text in that larger biblical story.

The **Suggestions for prayer and embodiment** build on the 'Thinking about' section and encourage you to explore further what the 'Focus text' could mean for you. In addition to providing invitations into prayer, imaginative reflection and embodiment of the text, alone and with groups, they also encourage other kinds of creative expression. Feel free to adapt these suggestions to suit you. Often you are invited to write, sketch, colour or paint, but add to those anything else that interests you: sculpture, dance, carpentry, photography, videography, baking, building, collage making, flower arranging, experimentation with glue, construction paper, and ribbon that you find in the bottom drawer or rocks you find in the garden.

As you create, give yourself permission to experiment freely in the way a small child would. The goal is not to do or make something perfect (although if you happen to be gifted at something, that is lovely). The goal is the experience of creation itself. See what happens and consider what that might tell you about God, the world or yourself.

Some of us may want to try all the exercises, to linger in the imaginative aspects and to take our time settling into a place of prayer. Others of us meet God best when we are active rather than reflective, and so selecting a single exercise, moving more quickly into the creative expression and choosing an activity that feels productive or practical might be most fruitful. Find what is best for you.

Consider collecting your notes and creative expressions so that you can review them at the end. You may wish to have a single notebook in which to record some of your reflections.

Individual exercises may be done in a group setting with time for contemplation followed by time for discussion. Exercises designed for groups may also be adapted for individuals.

The **Words to take with you** (Hosea 14.2) are phrases from the 'Focus texts', which are easy to remember, so you can slip them into the back pocket of your mind and then take them out and contemplate them as you go about your days (or chew on them, like Ezekiel, who is told in 3.1–3 to 'eat this scroll'). You can repeat them intentionally as a prayer or let them make themselves at home in the way that a piece of a melody will sometimes become our constant companion.

The **Poetry to pray**, drawn from Psalms, Proverbs, Song of Songs or Isaiah, reflects the theme or 'Focus text' or emerges from the 'Thinking about' section or exercises. Poetry is especially good for prayer because we connect to it on different levels simultaneously and because the images speak to us as much as the ideas. See the 'Praying the text' section above, and do this as it suits you and as time permits. As the instructions mention, you need not read all of the text that you share with God.

The five **Supplementary passages** also reflect the theme or emerge from the 'Thinking about' section; some of them are cited there or mentioned in the 'Suggestions for prayer and embodiment'. These will enrich your engagement with the 'Focus text' and demonstrate how the theme for the week plays out in other parts of Scripture. You may wish to pray these (or any) texts, but it is also fine simply to read them as extra food for thought as you go along.

Remember to treat this book as a guidebook. A guidebook might direct you to the Eiffel Tower and also tell you where to find the best hot chocolate on the Left Bank, but if you only want, or have time for, one of those, you can always look at a postcard of the Eiffel Tower while you enjoy your drink! You and the Holy Spirit will together make use of what is here to shape the experience that will most help you meet God in the story.

Suggestions for groups

The material offered here is suitable for meetings or mini-retreats and is appropriate for any time of year. If you wish to work through the book during Lent, Chapter 1 corresponds to Ash Wednesday week and Chapter 8 to Easter week, and you will meet for the Epilogue some time later. Monthly meetings spanning an academic year (or any eight- or nine-month period) would also work well.

A basic meeting could include: preparation for prayer, since all of the work with the text is prayerful (see again the 'Praying the text' section, parts 1–3); presentation of the 'Focus text', with some silence afterwards (see 'Praying the text', parts 5–6); selected 'Suggestions for prayer and embodiment'; discussion, which can emerge from the presentation of the text or from the exercises or be based on the 'Thinking about' section. A mini-retreat might also include: 'Poetry to pray'; presentation/discussion of 'Supplementary passages'; sharing of the 'Reading through Mark' with members of the group taking various parts; additional 'Suggestions for prayer and embodiment'.

Try to assign the opening presentation of the 'Focus text' in advance (preferably to a group rather than an individual) to give time for thought and preparation; in some chapters there are suggestions for ways to enrich this presentation. People need not memorize the text, only read and present it as creatively and lovingly as possible. Some may find this challenging; those people sometimes turn out to be the most surprisingly wonderful readers! You can find creative ways to include and encourage everyone without pressuring anyone unduly. Non-speaking parts are possible. Everyone brings something uniquely beautiful to the embodiment of God's good news. Many exercises offer ways of presenting texts other than reading aloud.

Ideally, group members will work through the chapters on their own before the meetings, but even if some do not, they will be able to participate; the initial reading/performance of the text will introduce it, and exercises centre on prayer and creative expression in which everyone can be involved. If some people have already done individual exercises that you do in the group, they can ponder those again or try other creative expressions of them.

In the Epilogue, you are encouraged to meet again to experience the whole of Mark together in some way. You could do this within the confines of the group, or you could invite others to be in the audience or to participate in the presentation itself. You will find suggestions for this in the Epilogue, but it is something to have in mind as you plan together.

You may also wish to share some of your individual creative expressions with one another or a larger group. You could do this as you go along or wait until the end and ask people to bring to the final Epilogue meeting anything they'd like to share.

Sharing the experience online

You are welcome to share your ideas, images and links to video clips. To be in conversation with others along the way, please visit <www.onthewayofthebeloved.com>.

1

Into the Wilderness

———•◆•◆•———

Focus text	Mark 1.1–15
Reading through Mark	Mark 1—2
Poetry to pray	Isaiah 40.1–5, 27–31
Supplementary passages	Matthew 1—2
	Luke 1.1—2.40
	John 1.1–18
	Isaiah 65.17–25
	Luke 4.16–21
Words to take with you	Prepare the way of the Lord.

———•◆•◆•———

THINKING ABOUT MARK 1.1–15

Beginnings

Beginnings move us. Every beginning we choose to make, however small, every shift of our attention, our energy, our bodies, our hearts towards something new, moves us towards a slightly different future.

Beginnings of stories also do something to us. If the first words can capture our attention long enough to draw us in, then the beginning will set us on our way in a certain direction with a certain sense of where we are and with inklings of where the story might be taking us.

'In the beginning', the biblical story opens with God. God speaks the story into being, calling order and life out of formlessness and chaos. Then, when Scripture talks of new beginnings, it is again always a question of what God will do – God creating new heavens and a new earth, God creating a people Israel, God creating a way where there is no way (Isaiah 65.17–25; 43.1–2, 16–21). God's creativity stirs at the centre of biblical beginnings.

And so the writers of the Gospels, as the stories of Jesus came to be called from the Greek word for 'good news',[1] also start there in one way or another, with God doing something new. They situate the good news of Jesus within the eternal love story of God and the world. Then they find ways to entice us into the story too.

The Gospel of John opens 'in the beginning' with a burst of glory and shows us the Word–Son before time at the heart of God, speaking insuppressible light into being. Then the Word is made flesh in the first-century person Jesus, heralded by the witness John, already preparing the way from the Gospel's earliest verses.

Matthew begins with a genealogy that sets Jesus' story at the summit of the story of Israel. Then the miraculous baby, who is himself God-with-us, is born. And we see the star and visitors from afar, a murderous king and innocent deaths, a flight into Egypt and Joseph's sacred dreams of angels.

Luke begins with a note to the most excellent reader, then takes us to the temple, where Gabriel foretells the birth of John. The stories of two impossible births made possible by God unfold to the cadences of prophetic poetry, echoing Israel's sacred stories of God's surprising abundance, justice and grace. And we see the manger, shepherds with their heavenly host, Mary pondering all these things in her heart.

Mark's particular telling has elements of all of these and yet, like each of them, is utterly distinctive.

Like John and Genesis, Mark opens with a beginning: 'The beginning of the good news of Jesus Christ, the Son of God.' It could be the title for the next 14 verses, it could be the title of the whole book, or it could be both things. Mark 1.1–15 certainly lays out a beginning, establishes a context, puts things in motion, does all the things a good beginning does. But there is a strong sense in which the whole book is also only a beginning with a future stretching out beyond it, all the way to us and beyond us into God's for ever.

After the opening pronouncement, Mark reaches back into God's promises to Israel. Through them, God speaks to the coming anointed

Son. Mark calls on Isaiah, and certainly if the church were to choose a single prophetic book that has most helped us find words for what Jesus means and to express our hopes for our future with him, it is that one. Mark 1.3 is drawn from Isaiah 40, which makes an appearance in the early chapters of all four Gospels, while Mark 1.2 has echoes of Exodus 23.20 and Malachi 3.1. So in two verses Mark evokes several memories of Israel's story and situates Jesus there, addressed by God already in 1.2, promising to send this messenger who will prepare the way. Then the messenger-baptizer John appears.

Along with God, Jesus and John, we ourselves seem to be invited into those first verses. That voice in the wilderness cries out through time: 'Prepare the way of the Lord, make his paths straight' (Mark 1.3).

And before we know it, we are in the wilderness, hearing John calling us to be made new. If we go out there with the crowds, if we stick with this story, which moves so quickly and with so much urgency that we can hardly stop ourselves, we will be part of Mark's beginning too.

There is no baby in this beginning. No human parents (although we will catch a glimpse of Mary and of brothers and sisters later). No manger, no star, no farmers from down the road or magi bearing costly gifts, no threatening king (not yet, but a shadow of one will fall over 1.14). Only God, a voice, a river and crowds of people responding to this prophet who brings back memories of Elijah. All of them are coming out with us to the baptizer preaching a turning towards God's new thing, an awakening for sleeping souls, a straightening of what is twisted, a release from all that binds for those who are willing to go out into the wilderness of new beginnings and meet God.

Then the one stronger than John appears at the Jordan, an adult Galilean emerging from that crowd of Judeans: Jesus, who we already know from Mark's introductory proclamation of holy goodness is the Anointed One, the Son of God.

The Son himself comes to take part in this mind-changing baptism, and Mark lets us see what the Son sees: the heavens torn apart (Isaiah 64.1). This is not an opening (as in Matthew 3.16 and Luke 3.21) like the opening of a lift door or a vault, where a tidy, complete closing is bound to follow, but an irreparable rending of the bounds of heaven and earth – a visible manifestation of God breaking through with his reign of powerful, heart-rending, heart-healing love that makes new.

Then the Spirit like a dove – perhaps as Gerard Manley Hopkins imagines it with 'ah! bright wings' – descends on the one who will baptize with the Holy Spirit.

Mark lets us overhear the voice of the heavenly parent speaking eternal love to this adult child: 'You are my Son, the Beloved; with you I am well pleased' (1.11).

The voice will return in 9.7 with a more public declaration of love and a command to disciples through the ages to listen to this beloved, Spirit-bearing Son. Then in 15.38, as Jesus cries out and breathes his last, the tearing of the temple curtain will signal again the heavenly breach, and in that moment a Roman officer will recognize the Son. But here at his beginning only Jesus sees and hears God's claim on him, as we watch through the window of Mark's words.

Then a strange thing happens. Mark cuts to the chase. We may not see it as strange any more because we know the story so well, but surely if we didn't already know it, this is not what we would expect.

After that beautiful, life-altering moment, Jesus doesn't return straightaway to Galilee trailing clouds of glory. The voice of divine love doesn't start him on a gentle way through life. Rather, God's love prepares him for a battle that he is uniquely able to undertake. It is the conflict behind all the work he'll do with all those crowds, all the sick and dying and demon-possessed, who begin to appear immediately in this first chapter. It is the conflict behind the opposition of the Pharisees with their ideas of how he should behave[2] and the fearful calculation of the chief priests, elders and scribes, who feel threatened to the point of murder, and the brutal work of the Roman soldiers, who finally kill him.

The assurance of divine love prepares Jesus to face the enemy who will stand behind all those challenges and speak through all of the unclean spirits, who populate the landscape of this Gospel more than any other. God's love descended on Jesus in the Spirit drives him out into the wilderness to bring God's best near, even in the face of the world's worst, to bring life where there is hopelessness, fear and despair.

Days of beasts and angels

The verb translated *drive out* in 1.12 is the same that will be used when Jesus *casts out* demons. In Luke and Matthew, the Spirit *leads*

Jesus out. But Mark's image is of a person thrust forward into God's love-fuelled battle for the soul of creation.

Then Satan tempts him. We all know it, but it is perhaps easy to forget that evil is not only cunning but can also be dreadfully appealing in its way. If it only repelled, it could not tempt. Matthew and Luke tell us the nature of this temptation. They suggest that Satan is tempting Jesus to take the golden path that you might think a heavenly blessing would open up. But Mark does not say.

We perhaps find clues in later references to Satan. He is in 4.15 the one who takes away the word that is sown in people, like birds eating seeds on a path, and so perhaps here he seeks to devour the word that is sown in the Son himself. Then in 8.33, when Peter rebukes Jesus after Jesus first tells his disciples that he will suffer and die and rise again, Jesus turns and rebukes Peter with the words: 'Get behind me, Satan! For you are setting your mind not on divine things but on human things.' So here in these days of temptation, perhaps Satan suggests, as Peter will later do, that the way that leads to the cross must be a terrible mistake.

But what Jesus knows, what we know, is that no path is golden without God and that God's path always is. Even if it doesn't look that way, particularly when our sight is dimmed by weariness or pain, still God's way holds the golden light of life in it.

Although Mark doesn't tell us about the temptations, he does give us a bit more information about the wilderness.

The word *wilderness* may evoke different things for different ones of us. For some of us, the wilderness is somewhere wonderful, holy and beautiful, where our souls are restored; and perhaps we might so imagine the first wilderness of 1.3–4, where the good news begins with the voice of God's messenger calling people out to him and the dove descending on the holy Son.

But there is another kind of wilderness that most of us know in one way or another. Sometimes it may be an actual place of lonely desolation where evil prowls. But it could also be a wilderness of the heart with personal beasts that creep in the corners of our minds and carve out territory in our nightmares and haunt foggy days of heartsickness. This wilderness of Jesus' temptation is surely that sort of place.

The word for the *beasts* of 1.13 appears only here in the Gospels, but it runs rampant in Revelation, appearing dozens of times to evoke the embodiment of evil (see, for example, Revelation 13 and 17).

So there are wild beasts in Jesus' wilderness.

But there are also ministering angels. Not only does he have the Spirit soaring in his soul and the memory of that voice, God's beautiful claim on him; he also has God's messengers.

The word I have translated *minister* – the angels *ministering* to him – is also translated *serve, wait on* or *provide for*. Later, in 1.31, after Jesus heals Simon's mother-in-law, she gets up right then and there and *serves* everybody. That is the same word. It is also used of the women at the cross in 15.41, where we hear that they used to follow him and *provide for* him in Galilee.

There is one more occurrence of this word, in 10.45. There we find that it is Jesus' own vocation: 'For the Son of Man came not to be served but to serve, and to give his life a ransom for many.'

So serving is no small thing, and it is comforting perhaps to know that Jesus, the beautiful servant par excellence, has minister-messengers of God attending him all along. *Messenger* is another way to translate the word for *angel*; it is the word in 1.2 for the messenger God sends to prepare Jesus' way. Even before the messenger-angels in the wilderness, there is John sent to make Jesus' paths straight, and then there are women, until the very end and even beyond it at his tomb, who serve him all along his way as the angels do here in these 40 days and nights.

Then he returns to Galilee (1.14). And now, we are told, John the Baptist has been arrested, and later we will learn that Herod has him executed (6.16). So even here in this first chapter, it is certainly never all easy. Even with God's love on the loose, the Spirit having flown through the bounds of heaven and earth for ever – even then good people die. The very best people even.

The word for *arrested* is also translated *betrayed* or *handed over* and is later used repeatedly of Jesus, betrayed by Judas, arrested by the religious authorities, handed over to Pilate, who hands him over to the Roman soldiers to be crucified. So in that brief whisper of bondage in 1.14 is foreshadowed the future of the Son and of his followers, who Jesus says will also be arrested, handed over and betrayed (13.9–12).

But that is never the last word. Satan has met the stronger man with the power to bind what is unclean and deathly. God's life and love make a way through even the worst. Jesus takes that way so that we can see. Even though we don't see the whole picture, we can see that beyond and even within the pain that we know is present in this life, God reigns, and the kingdom of God takes root and grows. And beyond the cross stands an empty tomb.

Following the preacher of God's good news

Here are a few things we might wish to contemplate about Jesus' beginning in Mark as we begin our own journey with him through the Gospel.

We might contemplate God's parental, eternal love breaking through anything that we imagine keeps God somewhere else. We might consider the Spirit's winged descent, the driving power that gives Jesus the will and the strength to face Satan. We might remember that Jesus has his time of temptation in his own wilderness, that it is real temptation in a real wilderness with wild beasts but that, even there, there are ministering angels.

Then we might ask: What about us?

We are not called to be little Jesuses. We don't have to be because he's already been Jesus, and by the power of the Holy Spirit he still does God's work in us, with us and for us.

And yet even in Mark, Jesus' story does not begin with him alone but with that voice crying in the wilderness and the ones who come to turn their lives around, to wake up to God's newness and love. Lots and lots of people go out there to the one preparing Jesus' way. We might find ourselves among them. We might find that we are also called, not just once but again and again, to turn and wake up and be more completely God's own, to *repent*.

The noun appears in Mark only in 1.4, in the baptism of *repentance* for the forgiveness of sins, which John is preaching. Then the verb appears in Jesus' first words in the Gospel, the summary of his preaching (1.15): 'The time is fulfilled. The kingdom of God is at hand.

Repent and believe [trust in, commit to, embody] the good news.' The verb *repent* appears one other time when Jesus' disciples also preach that all should repent (6.12).

John *preaches repentance* as a preparation of Jesus' way. Jesus *preaches repentance* as a response to the nearness of God's kingdom and a way into the good news. His disciples *preach repentance*. Then, when Jesus says that future believers will also preach (13.9–11), we might imagine that they (and we among them) will also *preach repentance*.

While repentance surely seems a lovely thing in those early verses of Mark where it emerges from the poetry of Isaiah as a way to prepare for the Lord and then is couched in God's best news, do we not sometimes find that our rendition of repentance gets mired in regret and shame and a profound sense of our failure? But repentance – *metanoia* in Greek, which means literally *a change of mind* – is not merely, or even primarily, a rehashing of our own past. It is a turning towards God's future for us, a fundamental shift in the direction of God's transforming love for us and for the whole world.

This obviously does entail a recognition that we are turning away from something. We know that we have our own particular brokenness. The very culture we inhabit, insofar as it is not leading us on paths of righteousness for his name's sake, is fundamentally flawed in ways that it does not fully recognize and in which we are complicit. Like the crowds of 1.5, we confess the truth about ourselves so that we can be wholly, authentically present to the One who seeks us. But listening for the call of God's love over the clamour of our own brokenness, responding honestly and then experiencing God's claim on us is surely all as joyous and profound as it is humbling and perhaps at times painful. It is a countercultural awakening to God's beautiful, ever-new otherness, which is embodied in Jesus and, by the power of the Holy Spirit, also in us.

The word for *forgiveness* (1.4) also means *release*; it appears in Jesus' mission statement in Luke 4.18 when Jesus is sent to proclaim *release* to the captives and to let the oppressed go *free*. Forgiveness of sins isn't God saying, 'Oh, that's all right. Now that you've told me that you know how awful you are and all the really wretched things you've done, I'll let it go.' It isn't us changing God's mind. It is God creating a change in ours. It is God releasing us from what binds us. God calls us into his love; we turn to God and away from all that we can discern is not God (which may sometimes happen in a giant transforming leap and sometimes in a halting, long, repetitive process); and God frees us from any power of un-lovingness within or outside ourselves. Perhaps we find that he released us long ago and that it is we who continued to cling blindly to bonds that were already broken. Or perhaps we find that we need to ask him to free us again and again because we are prone to wander, and God knows that.

The church recognizes this in the season of Lent, which is a time for awareness, a time for making space for God's goodness in our lives by turning away from all that is not that. But *metanoia* and release are not merely Lenten activities. They are part of the daily experience and embrace of God's love.

As we consider the repentance and forgiveness of Mark 1.1–15, we might be reminded of Romans 12.2 in which we are urged not to be conformed to this world but to be transformed by the renewing of our minds so that we may embody the good, acceptable and perfect will of God. That is precisely what Mark seems to be suggesting as well, that *metanoia* and holy release are not ends in themselves. We are made new so that we can prepare the way for Jesus in our lives and can then follow him into God's countercultural way.

But even then, even washed in the waters of God's steadfast love, as Jesus himself is, so we also may find ourselves sometimes in lonely wildernesses of our own, sometimes places not of our choosing – untamed places in the world or in our lives or in our own hearts where even we, although we are not little Jesuses whose saving work is for the whole world, even we may find ourselves tempted by the fool's gold of Satan. This will look different for each of us, but we can be certain that our temptation, like Jesus', will be fundamental; we will be tempted away from God's best for us, tempted to forget who we are, to forget the light in moments of darkness. And there may be wild beasts, which will look different for each of us too.

But also angels. If we think back, each of us can remember times when God has sent messengers to minister to us, feed us, care for us or look into our eyes with the complete acceptance that heals. Most of us can probably remember many times, if we try.

There is another connection too between Jesus' once-for-all moment and our smaller ones on our way with God, the most important one. It is that just as he is God's beloved Child, so also are we. We may not hear a voice from heaven, but the same Spirit who descends on Jesus works in us now to give us the blessed assurance of that love. We read it again and again in our sacred texts, and we hear it proclaimed Sunday after Sunday: God loves you with an everlasting love from which nothing, not the world's best or the world's worst, not Satan's cunning, not death, not anything, can separate you.

Like Jesus, we are not alone. Like him we are claimed.

As beloved children, we are also invited to be part of God's love. Jesus doesn't do God's will on earth with Satan in that wilderness and then quietly or triumphantly disappear. He proclaims God's good news in the world, and we hear him now today. 'The kingdom of God is at hand,' he tells us. Then his very next act in the Gospel is to call ordinary human beings like us to leave what they are doing and be part of what he is doing. They don't understand it, and they mess up again and again, but God works even in their failings to teach them and move them towards his purposes, not only for themselves but for others around them and for us now, who read about their struggles and see the long view of God in their lives as they follow.

And so we follow too. We follow through the wilderness and the glory, through our darkest and brightest moments, through the world's best and its worst. God's children. Jesus' brothers and sisters. On whom his Spirit descends with 'ah! bright wings' to lead us on God's golden way.

SUGGESTIONS FOR PRAYER AND EMBODIMENT

Mark calls us down to the water to pray. In Mark 1 we find the River Jordan, and the Sea of Galilee (a large lake, like a Highland loch or an American Great Lake), the only lake to appear regularly in Mark 1—8.

Think of a river or a lake that you have found beautiful – perhaps a favourite place in your life or in film or art. Go there in your mind's eye. Hear and see the water and the surroundings as you approach. What does the water sound like? What else do you hear? What does the air feel like? What time of day or night is it? Sit or lie comfortably and quietly beside it, alone or with people you love.

Now hear a compelling voice calling from a distance: 'Prepare the way of the Lord.' What might it mean for you in the current season of your life to do that? Pause and consider this question if you wish.

Now imagine Jesus speaking to you there at the waterside. What does his voice sound like? Is it familiar or unfamiliar? Does he speak in the accent of someone you love? Hear him inviting you to shift your attention to God's good news, which is bigger than all of the bad news in the world. Consider his invitation. What might it mean for you to turn around or wake up to God's love for you, then to step out and feel that God's love is solid ground for your soul? What might it mean for you to trust that the most important news in the world and in your life is, in fact, good?

Ponder one or all of the questions above, and stay with Jesus by the water for as long as you wish.

When you are ready, express your response to this waterside experience by writing, sketching, colouring, baking or carpentry (see p. ix for more ideas). For the purposes of this and every other invitation to creativity in this book, choose any medium of expression that appeals to you (or is at hand) when you do the exercise.

After you have created your response, see if it suggests anything new about yourself or about God's love for you. If you wish, return to the waterside and offer that to Jesus.

———•◆•———

Have you had the experience of feeling driven by the Spirit (or lifted by the scruff of your neck!) into or out of some situation in your life? Take some time to remember and express (write, sketch or other) how that felt. Is the Spirit driving you anywhere now? Can you see what that place looks like?

———•◆•———

Remember times when you have been in a wilderness place of some kind. Write, sketch or colour in as much detail as you wish what one (or several) of those experiences was like. Did you ever find, possibly against all expectations, that you came out of a painful or difficult wilderness time with a renewed sense of purpose? Would it help you to reconnect with that sense of purpose now?

———◆◆◆———

Who have been ministering angels to you? Take five minutes or more to list as many as you can remember. Some of these might be people very close to you; others might be people who crossed your path only once. After assembling your angels, if you feel comfortable doing so, write about, paint, sketch or mould from clay (or modelling dough) one or more images of wild beasts who have prowled in your life, who may even now inhabit your heart. Then write or sketch the story of the defeat or taming of the beast by your most powerful ministering angels as agents of God's love from which nothing can separate you.

———◆◆◆———

We are told in Scripture that in Christ we are all children of God. The tearing of the heavens implies that the breach between heaven and earth is irreparable, that God is now with us, that his love is on the loose. In the voice of a person you love and trust, hear God saying to you now: 'You are my beloved child.' Now hear the words in as many loving voices as you can remember, one after another. Take as long as you like to rest in this.

———◆◆◆———

They say that Martin Luther, the great reformer of the church, if he was struggling, would sometimes put his hand on his head and say, 'I am baptized.' Pass a small bowl of water around the group (this would work well before the opening time of stillness in your first meeting), or do this on your own and speak the words to yourself. Dip your fingers in the water, place your hand on the top of your head, hold it there gently, and consider that you have been claimed as a child of God. Pass the bowl to the person beside you and address that person by name: 'John, you are beloved.' (If you are doing this alone, you might combine it with the previous exercise and hear the

loving voices you heard there as you hold your hand on your head.)
After you explain this exercise, ask people to say their names as a
reminder. Then begin by addressing the first person and handing her
the bowl: 'Jane, you are beloved.'

----•◆•----

When you have the reading/performance of Mark 1.1–15 in your
group meeting, pause at the end to allow everyone time to hear the
call to prepare the way of the Lord and to sit with Jesus' first words
and consider how they might wish to respond. You could use the first
exercise above for this purpose.

----•◆•----

Divide into sub-groups and, in your sub-group (or on your own if
you are working through Mark alone), develop an interpretation of
one or more episodes in Mark's account of the beginning of Jesus'
ministry: 1.16–20; 1.21–28; 1.29–31; 1.32–34; 1.35–39; 1.40–45; 2.1–12;
2.13–17; 2.18–22; 2.23–28. This could be a single image you form
with your bodies or a series of images, perhaps using simple props.
It could be a retelling of the events from the perspective of one
character, for which you could adapt the story to your own context.
It could be a reading/performance in which you invite others to
participate, as scribes, disciples, crowds, tax collectors, sinners and
so on. It could be very brief, just a single image, or it could take
longer – whatever creates an experience of that episode. Offer your
mini-performances to the rest of the group in the order in which they
appear in Mark.

2

Following the Teacher

Focus text	Mark 4
Reading through Mark	Mark 3—4
Poetry to pray	Proverbs 8.1–11, 22–31
Supplementary passages	Matthew 5.1–12
	Luke 11.1–13
	John 13.12–17
	1 Corinthians 2
	Ephesians 3.14–21
Words to take with you	To you has been given the secret of the kingdom of God.

THINKING ABOUT MARK 4

The teacher and the secret

If someone were to ask us what springs to mind when we consider Jesus' teaching, we might first think of Matthew's Sermon on the Mount or Luke's memorable parables of the prodigal son and the good Samaritan or John's discourses on the vine and the shepherd. We might not most associate Mark with Jesus as teacher.

But Mark actually does present Jesus as a great and constant teacher, as the very ideal of what a teacher is.

We know from experience that we learn not only by what teachers say but also by the sorts of people we perceive them to be – teachers in the broadest sense of the word, including our parents, partners and friends who teach us many things, but also professional teachers. The best teachers demonstrate what they want us to learn, and sometimes it is our love for the teacher that inspires in us a love for the subject. Jesus is that sort of teacher, and what he demonstrates is the goodness, justice and power of the kingdom of God – or *reign* of God, as it is sometimes called, because it isn't so much a place as a way of living in the world.

In Jesus' first appearance after he calls his first disciples, he teaches in the synagogue (1.21–28). Already there the authority of his teaching overflows into an act that demonstrates the inbreaking of God's reign. The good news and its manifestations are all of a piece in Mark. Jesus, the teacher, casts out an unclean spirit, and the crowd in 1.27 responds: 'What is this? A new teaching – with authority!' The crowds may never understand fully who he is (although the unclean spirits do, 1.24), but they seem always to understand that his teaching and his deeds of power come as a package (see also 6.2), and so they repeatedly come to the teacher expecting him not only to tell them something but to do something for them: '*Teacher*, I brought you my son,' says the desperate father of 9.17; '*My teacher*, let me see again,' says Bartimaeus in 10.51.

Jesus is always teaching. He teaches in synagogues (1.21; 6.2), by the sea (2.13; 4.1; 6.34), in homes (2.2), in villages (6.6), on the way (8.31; 9.31; 10.17) and in the temple (11.17; 12.35; 14.49). He teaches great crowds (4.1; 6.34; 10.1); he teaches his closest followers in private (4.34; 13.5–37); he teaches his enemies (3.22–30; 6.2–6; 11.27—12.27). His teaching is authoritative (1.27), compassionate (6.34), simultaneously astounding and offensive (6.2–3), spellbinding (11.18), fearless (in that he does it boldly in the face of opponents who will kill him, 11.17–18), mysterious (4.11–12) and pleasurable (12.37). It inspires commitment, awe, confusion, homicidal rage and delight. And none of that matters to him.

He does not seek to be liked, and he does not expect everyone to agree with him or to respond positively. He knows that they will not (4.11–12). His teaching is both not at all about him and entirely about him; paradoxically he does not factor into the equation at all and yet is at the centre of it. His immense love for God and neighbour issues in a commitment to the good news of the kingdom of God so complete that while he is constantly teaching this news, he is also always embodying it fully in life and in death with extravagant, life-altering, enraging, exquisite, heart-rending generosity. His disciples (or students, as it might be helpful to put it) are meant to learn not only by listening to what he says but also by watching how he lives.

Mark 4 vividly displays for us the story of Jesus as teacher, the essence of his teaching about the kingdom, and the way in which the kingdom manifests itself not only in his words but also in his person.

The parable of the sower (4.3–20) begins with invitations to listen and look (although 'look' is missing from the NRSV), and so we hear the word and also see it unfold before our eyes in images of seeds and birds, rocks and thorns, and ultimately abundant fruitfulness.

But then we are told that however vivid and evocative the images might be, they were never intended to be enough (4.10–12). God's good news is not on offer as a sound bite. It is on offer as a relationship. And so God's plan is that the teaching comes with the teacher. God wraps the teaching in a mystery (the word for *secret* in 4.11 is the basis for our word *mystery* and can also be translated that way: 1 Corinthians 2.1; 15.51) so that we cannot turn our hearts towards an easy, incomplete truth.

But the secret is there; the sower-Jesus spreads the word liberally. He speaks it over and over in every way, every context, to every crowd, every soul who gets within hearing distance of him. He keeps speaking it even when he is in danger of being crushed by the crowds so that finally he has to sit on a boat on the sea while he addresses the multitude on the land.

Some of that multitude will not even take it in before Satan swoops in to steal it. Some will react with a happy, shallow faith that fails them when hardship presses on their hearts. Some will be fatally distracted by worry or enchanted by wealth or lost in a world of desire for all that does not satisfy.

Even his own disciples cannot grasp the mystery in its fullness until they have followed him all along the hard way to the cross and seen the future beyond the empty tomb; most of them fall away before the bitter end. The word he uses when he tells his disciples in 14.27 that they will all *become deserters* is used in 4.17 of the ones who receive the word on rocky soil and immediately *fall away* when the going gets tough. But he also promises in 14.28 that there will be more to come. The disciples' failure will not be the end. He will be raised, and they will see him again. We know that eventually they got it. They did bear fruit 'thirty and sixty and a hundredfold' (4.20) once they had experienced and embodied the whole glorious substance of God's countercultural good news.

Jesus' word may be met with threefold failure, and even the hearts of some of the ones closest to him who are offered the treasure of his presence all along his way may struggle to grasp it, may listen but not understand and look but not perceive (8.17–18). But what the Son knows is that this is no reason to despair because God's abundance is inevitable. There may yet be hope even for the ones on the path and on the rocks and in the thorns. For all of us.

When the lamp 'comes' is literally what Jesus says in 4.21. When the lamp comes, will its light not shine for all to see? Despite all appearances to the contrary, despite all the rocks and thorns in the world, this secret will be revealed in God's good time. The light of the world will not be contained.

The kingdom, like Jesus' teaching, may be underground for now, but it is quietly taking root, as the next two parables teach.

Abundant, sheltering grace

Building on the parable of the sower, the pair of little parables of the kingdom of God in 4.26–32 suggest again that, like the parable form itself, the kingdom may be hidden from those unaware of its secret presence, but it is also destined to be revealed in its fullness and produce a harvest.

The first parable of the kingdom (4.26–29) is again a story of sowing and harvesting. The sower sows, then sleeps and rises, night and day, as step by step the kingdom grows, invisibly at first and then in the form of a stalk, then the head, then the full grain in the head. The word for *grain* in 4.29 may also be translated *fruit* (as in Galatians 5.22 and the vine metaphor of John 15). So while this is about the natural progression of rising wheat, it is also an image of fruitfulness.

We know from the earlier parable that some seed will not be fruit-ful, but in this image as in the earlier one we are encouraged not to worry too much about that. We cannot control what happens after the word is sown. We just sow it. Only that. The sower here does not even weed or water, just sows and waits in peaceful trust.

Then the one who is over all *sends in the sickle* when the time is right; that is the literal translation of the phrase translated *goes in with his sickle* in the NRSV. The implication is that God or Jesus (the ones who normally do any significant sending) will manage the kingdom harvest. If there is room for us to plant the seeds of the word, for the rest, we, along with the sower of the parable, can leave that to God.

So this kingdom garden is no ordinary garden. Keen gardeners know the constant effort required to keep things under control, particularly when rainy British summers cause an overwhelming explosion of growth. And we may sometimes feel that God's kingdom requires that sort of hopeless effort. We may begin to believe that the kingdom is ours rather than God's to grow. But these parables suggest that we don't really do any of the heavy lifting. We aren't in charge. In the parable, the sower admits that he does not know how it happened. Nor do we. God's ways of entering human hearts and calling them to him are mysterious and beyond our imagining or our control.

On the other hand, we are invited to do something. We scatter the seed. In word and deed we embody and share our good news. We 'tell the old, old story of Jesus and his love', as the old hymn puts it. But we don't fret about the future of the kingdom or about the future of our church or about our own future in the loving arms of God. The kingdom, the church and our hearts are all in God's capable hands. We do our part as beautifully, lovingly, invitingly and completely as we know how. Then we trust, and we watch for God's gardening grace.

Like the first parable, the second parable (4.30–32) illustrates the growth of the kingdom from something hidden and minute to something fully visible, but it also hints at more features of God's reign. The mustard plant presents the contrast between the smallness of the present kingdom and the relative largeness of it in its fullness. This kingdom will grow generously and abundantly from the smallest of all seeds to the largest of all shrubs.

In a similar parable in Luke 13.18–19 and Matthew 13.31–32, the shrub magically becomes a tree in which the birds build nests; we find a similar image of a cedar in Ezekiel 17.22–24. But Mark's mustard plant stays a mustard plant. This word for *shrub* is translated *vegetable* and *herb* elsewhere in the NRSV. So the mustard plant, though a very big shrub, is not a giant thing like a cedar. In this parable, Jesus chooses a common plant to describe how the kingdom could be working its way into something amazingly large from the tiniest whisper of a beginning. But he doesn't use an amazingly large object to make the point. He uses the image of a bird nesting in the shade of a bush. It is an image of expansive gentleness but not of overwhelming, unmissable glory. The kingdom of God is described not in grandiose terms but in terms of ordinary, quiet beauty as an inviting place to call home.

So we can look for and recognize signs of the presence of God's reign among us in the ordinary, quietly beautiful blessings of our lives. God grants his abundant grace in the small and the gentle just as surely as in the magnificent and the vast.

There is a summary statement at the end of the passage (4.33–34): 'With many such parables he spoke the word to them, as they were able to hear it; he did not speak to them except in parables, but he explained everything in private to his disciples'. This echoes what we read about parables earlier in the chapter. All are included in Jesus' teaching, but as the kingdom gestates and sprouts, staying near to Jesus and his way, turning to him day by day, listening for his guidance and resting in his love puts us in a position to learn more about the kingdom so that we don't miss the quiet growth of the familiar mustard plant in our own garden or indeed the seeking presence of others around Jesus, wanting, like us, to nest in the shade of his fruitful, abundant, sheltering grace.

The parables of Mark 4 as a whole emphasize the hiddenness and smallness of the beginnings of the kingdom. We may not be able always to imagine how God is working in us to bring about the harvest of his good news in the world. We may not even notice the tiny sprouts or be aware of the hidden seeds that we have planted now taking root. The parables also underscore the sense in which we do not make the kingdom happen by force of will. The sower just sows and then gets a good night's sleep, and the earth produces of itself, and the mustard plant puts forth its large branches. The kingdom grows organically. Then, inevitably, as day follows night, God's hidden, mysterious work in the world and in us will be fruitful. And not just a little fruitful – God's grace is not meagre but abundant. God is not worried. And so we needn't be either.

Even when the storms come.

To the other side

After this day when he's been teaching parables of the kingdom of God from a boat because there are so many people on the shore, Jesus turns to the ones on board with him and says, 'Let us go across to the other side.' And they leave the crowd behind and set out across the sea.

Jesus' crossings are more than geographical. Jesus crosses many social and spiritual boundaries. He eats with unsuitable people. He breaks Sabbath laws. He associates with the unclean and heals them at the wrong times. He communicates with unclean spirits.

As Jesus and his student-disciples are crossing to the other side of the Sea of Galilee, they are also crossing other boundaries, into Gentile territory, where they will be met immediately by a person possessed by a legion of demons rushing at Jesus from the tombs. Then the next sea crossing 21 verses later takes Jesus into an encounter with the silent desperation of a suffering woman and the chaotic grief of a household in which a little girl has died, and in both cases Jesus touches people who would have been considered ritually unclean.

For us too, we can expect that being schooled by this teacher will mean leaving the crowd behind metaphorically as the disciples leave it literally in this passage. It will mean looking at things in a different way, caring about people that society does not necessarily care about, noticing and reaching out in love to the vulnerable, the lonely, the superficially unlovely, the poor and the weak, not just the wealthy, powerful, gifted and conventionally beautiful, whom we are often encouraged to admire and respect. Leaving the crowd behind and following Jesus can mean finding ourselves in unexpected places, which can be challenging for us, as it was for those first disciples.

Crossing to the other side with Jesus may be a risky, unpredictable proposition, and in this passage, the wind and the sea create a visual manifestation of the dangers of being in the boat with him.

We all know that being a friend of Jesus, one of 'his own' (John 13.1), does not mean a storm-free life. Storms, internal ones and external ones, come to every life. No amount of preparation, money or goodness can keep them away. Those things can help certainly, whether you are a follower of Jesus or not. But they don't make life a cakewalk because being human is a complicated thing. Our bodies are fragile. People we love will certainly die. We will get sick and die ourselves. The unexpected will happen no matter how careful and good we are. For some of us, even the best and most prepared, these hardships will be very great indeed. Following Jesus does not prevent hardships from happening. We all know this to be true.

But here is what is different for us as his followers. Even when our lives or hearts are stormy or our way is hard or our minds are foggy, we have the blessed deep-down assurance that he's there, for us and for the world. We know that his love is wrapped around us no matter what. Even when we walk through the utter blackest darkness, even there his hand shall lead us and his right hand shall hold us fast.

We also know that we can turn to him honestly. Like the Psalmists, models of honest complaint (see especially Psalm 107.28–29 and the cries to God to wake up), we don't have to pretend that everything is all right or that we aren't angry or that we are blind to the suffering of the world. Jesus doesn't pretend those things. He walks straight across every boundary to meet that suffering head on. So we can be honest, as the disciples are honest in this story:

'Teacher, do you not care that we are perishing?' (4.38).

The word for *perishing*, or *being destroyed*, appears in 3.6, where the Pharisees are conspiring to *destroy* Jesus. It also appears in 8.35: 'Those who want to save their life will *lose* [*destroy*] it, and those who *lose* their life for my sake, and for the sake of the gospel, will save it.' The dangers of perishing are real, but taking the risky way of Jesus – the way of faith, hope and love – turns out paradoxically to be the safest, most life-affirming option.

Here the sleeping Jesus wakes to rebuke the wind and tell the sea to simmer down (4.39); the first word ('Peace!') is a verb meaning *be silent*; the second ('Be still!') means literally *be muzzled*. The word for *rebuke* – when Jesus rebukes the wind – is used when Jesus rebukes the unclean spirits elsewhere, including the first exorcism in 1.25. The unclean spirit there is also told to be muzzled (1.25). Then, after that first exorcism, the crowd marvels that even the unclean spirits obey this one who teaches with authority, as here the disciples marvel that even the wind and the sea obey their teacher. *'What* is this?' the crowd asks after that first encounter with an unclean spirit (1.27): 'A new teaching – with authority.' *'Who* is this?' ask the disciples here (4.41) who now understand that it is not just something about Jesus' teaching. It is something about who this teacher actually is.

The resemblance to exorcism emphasizes the extent of the threat in this story and also suggests that Jesus' effective rebuke of the wind and the sea is another instance of his power over all evil. His teaching of the kingdom word is authoritative because the kingdom is most powerfully at hand in him.

So this story, and every story, turns out really to be about who Jesus is. That is the point of the larger story of Mark, and it is the point of a life of discipleship. The point isn't us; it is him. And this realization can be surprisingly freeing when we are experiencing stormy seas – outside us or inside us.

But it might not always be what we expect or think we want. Although Jesus is in the deepest, most meaningful, most powerful sense our beloved friend, he is not just our pal. A pal in the boat would probably be right there with the others helping them get the ship back to shore or encouraging them. But Jesus is not.

They have to wake him up. And then he has a word with the sea and the wind, and he does still the storm, but he does not then say, 'There, there. Sorry to have worried you. Are you all right now?' Instead he says, 'Why are you afraid? Have you still no faith?'

And they are taken aback. The translation says that they are 'filled with great awe' (4.41, NRSV). But the Greek literally says that they 'feared a great fear'. Then they say, 'Who then is this, that even the wind and the sea obey him?'

In Mark 6.45–52, a passage with many parallels to this one, the disciples have another chance to experience the power of Jesus over the winds. There, as here, they have left a crowd behind and set out in a boat, at Jesus' command, for the other side. It is again evening, and where Jesus is asleep in our passage today, in 6.47 he is on the shore in prayer. But he sees when his own are struggling and comes to them, walking on the sea. As he gets into the boat with them, the wind ceases, and again they do not understand. Then there, as here after this first stormy crossing, what they find on the other side are suffering people, rushing at Jesus from every direction and then reaching out to touch his clothes.

Following Jesus may well take us straight into storms and struggles and the worst pain and suffering of the world. It may disorientate us, not once but repeatedly. But it also puts us in a position to experience reorientation towards life and away from fear; to witness and be part of his embrace of the broken and the marginalized; and to see his transformation of deathliness into fruitfulness.

Being in the boat puts us in a position to learn who Jesus, our teacher, is and to become more like him in our attitudes and our hopes.

Perhaps knowing what we know as followers who have already seen the end of Jesus' story and its new beginning (which the disciples at this point in their story have not), perhaps we, who celebrate the empty tomb and the resurrection glory and the pouring out of the Spirit, can recognize even in the midst of the fiercest storms of life, even before the healing and restoration and the blessed stillness, the presence of the one who is Lord of all nature and binder of Satan, this one who is with us even to the end of the age, brooding over us and the world, with peace and power and healing in his wings.

Then, carriers of the secret of the kingdom, we can cross to the other side and scatter the word generously, graciously, abundantly wherever it has yet to be planted, and we can watch as our gardener-God makes our smallest of all the seeds on earth blossom and grow.

SUGGESTIONS FOR PRAYER AND EMBODIMENT

Consider a parable or teaching of Jesus that has always been special to you or one that particularly comes to mind now. Sit with your memory of that teaching for a few minutes and consider what Jesus might be teaching you today. Then find the passage and read or pray it; if you don't know where it is, try an online concordance or ask a friend. Does anything new strike you – about the teaching, Jesus, yourself or the world?

We regularly pray for God's kingdom to come (Luke 11.2). Select one of the two kingdom parables in Mark 4 or some teaching about the kingdom in another Gospel (one of my favourites is Matthew 13.44), and pray that text (see 'Praying the text', p. vi). What does your passage suggest to you about the kingdom?

Consider what image or parable you might use for the kingdom now, perhaps something that is part of your daily life. Sketch, write, colour, paint or dance your kingdom image, or find images online or in a magazine that reflect what you have in mind and make a collage (for more ideas, see again p. ix).

As you pray Mark 4.1–34, imagine yourself on a boat with Jesus – perhaps a fishing boat with the smells and tools of that trade. Feel yourself in his presence and hear his voice speaking the parables. Then sit in silence with him, and consider what it means that he claims you not only as his student but also as his brother or sister (3.34–35; 1 John 3.1–2).

When Jesus begins to teach in Mark 4.3, he says, 'Listen!' Then, although it is not translated in the NRSV, he also says, 'Look!' ('Behold!' in the KJV). So we are invited both to hear and to see the parables. Divide into sub-groups, and in your sub-group (or on your own at home) select a parable section of Mark 4 and together create an image or a series of images with your bodies to express something about that passage. Share these with the rest of the group and take a couple of minutes in silence after each one for reflection. You might wish to take some time to share as a group what the process of forming the images opened up for you or what you saw in another group's image that revealed something in the passage that you had not noticed before or that prompted a new thought about Jesus and the kingdom.

———————•◦•◦•———————

As a group, in sub-groups or on your own, consider ways in which you or people you know have been affected by actual meteorological storms, as the disciples are in 4.35–41. Then consider metaphorical storms that have just as violently affected you in your body or your heart or that might be affecting you now, or perhaps storms in the life of your church; you may wish to share these or to consider these privately. Have you been aware of Jesus 'in the boat' with you? Has he ever seemed to be asleep?

In the presentation of the passage (or a rereading), when you reach the line 'Teacher, do you not care that we are perishing?', read that as a group. Pause to consider your personal storms and offer those to God. Then continue the reading and hear Jesus speaking to your storm: 'Peace! Be still!' When you reach 4.41, join in reading together: 'Who then is this, that even the wind and the sea obey him?'

Follow this with a time of silence and, if you wish, bring the question to Jesus: 'Who then are you?'

3

Following the Healer

———•◆•———

Focus text	Mark 5
Reading through Mark	Mark 5.1—6.29
Poetry to pray	Psalm 13
Supplementary passages	Matthew 11.28–30
	Romans 8.35–39
	Ezekiel 37.1–14
	Matthew 25.34–40
	2 Corinthians 4.7–10
Words to take with you	Go in peace.

———•◆•———

THINKING ABOUT MARK 5

Hearing the healing in Mark

The teacher on the boat of Mark 4 has crossed over to the other side. Beyond the stormy seas, he is confronted by the torment of human suffering in its various guises: the raging of a tortured demoniac, the desperation of the father of a dying child, the silence of a woman carrying a dozen heavy years of pain, and then the quiet death chamber of a little girl.

Mark seems to have a heart for suffering people. We find throughout this Gospel a particular sensitivity to the pain of the world. When the Gospel is experienced in a performance or reading of the whole, rather than studied in silence or read aloud in small doses in worship, the space given to images and sounds of suffering is particularly striking.

Again and again, from the beginning of Jesus' ministry, crowds of the sick and demon-possessed cluster around him (1.32–34, 45; 2.1–4; 3.7–12, 20), and again and again in the stories of individuals, as we notice particularly in Mark 5, the narrative attends to their pain in a way that mirrors Jesus' compassionate attention to them.

The cries of the suffering stretch across Mark – from the loud voice of the demon bursting into the narrative in 1.26, which will be echoed in cries of recognition by unclean spirits wherever Jesus goes (unclean spirits are mentioned more than twice as many times as the Holy Spirit in Mark), to the urgent cries of Bartimaeus (10.47–48), and finally the cries of Jesus himself from his cross (15.34–37).

Mark makes space for the pain of the world and also for the agony of the crucifixion, with the account of Jesus' passion encompassing two chapters and the resurrection only eight verses. Even in Jesus' predictions of his death and resurrection (8.31; 9.31; 10.33–34), the suffering lingers in our minds such that the statements are typically called only 'passion predictions' even though, in every case, the resurrection is also predicted.

The second half of the Gospel emphasizes Jesus' teaching about the suffering that will mark his own mission and that of his followers. But even in the Gospel's first eight chapters, the sounds of the suffering of the world already point forward to the great cry of lament on the cross. Throughout Mark 5, in the deep transformations in the lives of these sufferers, there are intimations of the passion and resurrection to come, such that the Gospel creates a balance throughout between suffering and release, rejection and redemption, death and new life.

This balance in the world within the text also makes space in the world in front of it for the experience of hearers of this good news for whom the hard things in life sometimes loom large. In the midst of suffering, some may find it easier to take in the good news of divine love once it is clear that God hears our bad news too and that Jesus does not shirk or avoid suffering, unloveliness and brokenness but always moves towards sufferers in love.

Attending to the suffering in Mark creates space for us to acknowledge our own brokenness of body, mind and heart. It invites us to reach out to the Healer with our loud cries or breathless hopes or silent, searing need. Then perhaps we can hear carried in Jesus' great cry of lament from the cross echoes of all of the great cries of abandonment in the world, and see in the empty tomb God's eternal answer to them and us.

The person from the tombs who became a preacher

As soon as Jesus steps out of the boat into the country of the Gerasenes in 5.2, the absolute otherness of a company of demons runs at him. Their suffering host is unnamed and initially ungendered, described only as 'from the tombs a person in an unclean spirit'. The human being appears to have been 'swallowed up'[1] by evil, the self lost.

With the repeated reference to the tombs (5.2–5), their deathliness seems to cling to the sufferer: he comes from the tombs; he lives among the tombs; he howls among the tombs. The scene is also strewn with shackles and chains (5.3–4) as we hear of repeated attempts to bind the man until finally no one has the strength to try again.

The reference to the *strength* of the Gerasene evokes for us two earlier references to Jesus' battle with demonic forces. First, in 1.7, immediately before Jesus' baptism and meeting with Satan in the wilderness, John refers to Jesus as the *stronger* man who is coming after him, the one who will baptize with the Holy Spirit. Then in 3.27 when the scribes accuse Jesus of casting out demons by the power of Beelzebul, he says that before the *strong* man's (Satan's) house can be plundered, the *strong* man must be bound. So we are already aware from those references and from earlier accounts of Jesus' exorcisms that Jesus is the stronger man; we know that if no one else is strong enough to bind the forces that torture this Gerasene, Jesus certainly is. But while we may know this, the narrative does not rush to resolution. Rather, Mark emphasizes the extent and intensity of the suffering.

Night and day, the cries of the sufferer echo among the tombs and on the mountains. This *night and day* of relentless pain contrasts starkly with the gently rhythmic sleeping and rising *night and day* of the sower in 4.27, who peacefully observes the kingdom's growth. The Gerasene does not seem to sleep but only to suffer. We also learn in this verse that the repeated attempts to bind him were not because he was hurting others; these are the howls of a person who has turned the stones against himself in a relentless tumult of self-harm.

The tombs and stones and struggle of this passage might evoke for us the later tombs and stones in the Gospel. There are references to only two other tombs in Mark: those of John (6.29) and Jesus (15.46; 16.2–5). Both John and Jesus will also be bound as the Gerasene has been bound again and again. And the stones here might remind us of the one placed at the door of Jesus' tomb. Mark 5 is sprinkled with the rhetoric of passion and resurrection, quietly pointing us forward to the greater suffering and greater resolution of the Son of God in his larger struggle with Satan.

The Gerasene's demons know Jesus, as demons in Mark always do, and beg him not to torture them. Jesus asks their name, and then we learn the full measure of this man's oppression from within. He has not a single demon but an occupying force, a legion – a military image evoking the Roman occupation of Palestine and, with the drowning of the swine, perhaps also Israel's salvation story at the Red Sea with the slaves crossing to freedom as the powerful Egyptian force is engulfed behind them.

The demonic multitude begs Jesus not to send them out of the country and asks to enter the swine, who have been living alongside them on the hillside. Jesus gives them permission, and then the swine charge over a cliff to their death in the sea.

We might expect the story to end there, but it doesn't. The demons are destroyed, but the Gerasene's transformation is not yet complete. The narrative turns first to the reaction of the witnesses. The swineherds flee and tell the tale, and everyone comes to Jesus and sees the person, now clothed and in his right mind; the one they have bound again and again, to no avail, is now free. They are disorientated by his new orientation. For them this is not a cause for rejoicing. Instead they are afraid.

Like the demons who begged and begged, these people now also beg repeatedly – for Jesus to leave their neighbourhood.

As Jesus is getting back on the boat, the Gerasene who had met him as he stepped out is there again, this time asking to go with him. Instead, Jesus sends him home to his friends to build his new life. He is to go and tell what God's love has done in him. He does go, but he does more than tell the story to his family and friends: he begins to preach in the Decapolis (the NRSV translates it *proclaims*, but it is the word used of the preaching of Jesus, John and the disciples), and not just about God's mercy. He preaches Jesus, coming near to him, freeing him, transforming him. He finds his voice, and now he is no longer a source of fear or revulsion, no longer a tomb-dweller cloaked in unclean deathliness. He is now a bearer of good news. And everyone is amazed.

There are seven verses describing the Gerasene's plight before we hear Jesus' response, and there are 19 verses before the person's transformation is complete and he begins his new life of holy proclamation in 5.20. If we compare this story of the Gerasene with the parallel text in Matthew 9.18–26, we notice that Matthew's account focuses exclusively on Jesus' act of power while Mark's also tells the story of the transformation in the life of the suffering person.

We might be reminded of the psalms of lament, like Psalm 13, this chapter's 'Poetry to pray'. These psalms are called *psalms of lament, darkness* or *disorientation* precisely because the weight of the suffering is so great that, even though these psalms almost always end with restoration and an affirmation of God's faithfulness, we are left with a strong impression of the suffering that preceded it. Similarly, in Mark, the account of Jesus' healing and restoration is all the more moving because the narrative makes clear that his compassionate power enters into places of great, enduring and hopeless suffering.

Fearfully faithful

Jesus crosses the sea again (5.21), leaving behind the Gentile territory of tombs and swine, and again he is met by the great crowds that pressed him into the boat in 4.1. As the Gerasene appeared with his legion on the other side, now his opposite appears at Jesus' feet. Where the Gerasene was nameless and initially ungendered, Jairus has respectability (he is a leader of the synagogue) and a name. But this cannot save him from the desperation that he lays at Jesus' feet. He begs him repeatedly as the demons and the witnesses have begged him before, as desperate people have no doubt been begging Jesus since his first appearance in that synagogue in Capernaum. Jairus' words emerge with breathless agony (5.23): his daughter is dying; Jesus must come, lay hands on her, save her, let her live. Then he and Jesus set off through the crowd towards the dying little girl.

On a number of occasions in Mark we find one episode interrupted by another, and we watch the second episode play out while the first proceeds at a distance or is left suspended. Here the interruption comes in the form of a woman. In these Markan interruptions (called 'intercalations' and sometimes compared to a sandwich), we find that the two episodes shed light on one another in some way. As the woman appears and her story takes centre stage in 5.25–34, we listen for links, and we keep listening when Jairus' story starts up again in 5.35.

As Jairus was the Gerasene's opposite, so this woman is entirely unlike either of them. Unnamed, female and hidden in the crowd, she does not appear at all. She follows along behind, waiting for an opportunity to reach through the masses and touch Jesus' clothes. But first we hear about her flow of blood in what is one long sentence in Greek (5.25–27). The woman's suffering comes out in a rush of subordinate clauses, tumbling out in an endless flow of pain and loss, something like this: a woman, being in a flow of blood for 12 years and suffering much under many doctors and having spent all she had and having not grown better but rather worse, hearing about Jesus, coming in the crowd behind him (and finally we reach the main verb), *touched* his cloak, for she was saying, 'If I can touch his clothes, I shall be made well.'

And she is. Immediately the relentless eking away of her life, which has also left her destitute, ceases. She knows in her body that she has been freed from what is called here literally the *scourge* (5.29; see also 3.10), as anyone who has experienced or witnessed a long illness can understand.

As in the story of the Gerasene with its tombs and stones, so here also we hear faint echoes of the story of Jesus himself and his good news of life that must first pass through Gethsemane and Golgotha. Having heard now of the *blood* (5.25, 29) and *body* (5.29) of this woman, we will discover as we hear the rest of Mark that the only other body and blood to be mentioned will be Jesus' own: his *body* and his *blood* broken and poured out and given at the Last Supper (14.22, 24); his *body* anointed by the nameless woman with her

31

alabaster jar (14.8); his *body* requested by Joseph for burial (15.43). And no one else will be said to *suffer* (5.26) except the Son of Man himself (8.31; 9.12). So again we find in the suffering and healing of these people hints of the great suffering and rising of the Son, who will hold in himself the suffering and salvation of the whole world.

We do not know exactly the nature of her gynaecological complaint. Both of the phrases used to describe it are also used in passages in Leviticus related to uncleanness, so in addition to the suffering of the illness itself (which is not explained, but we might imagine pain, infertility, weakness, sorrow), she may also have suffered the social isolation of uncleanness. Scholars are in disagreement as to the precise nature of that isolation, and that is not the primary thrust of the passage. (There are no religious authorities popping up to complain, for example, as there are in passages focused primarily on Jesus' transgressions of religious laws; see 2.1—3.6.) We are not told the reason for her hiddenness and fear, but we can see that they figure in her suffering in some way and that they are reflections of pain.

As the story of the Gerasene was not finished when his demons were engulfed in the abyss of the sea, so this woman is not left to drift away invisibly in the crowd. When she knows in her body that she is healed, Jesus also knows that healing power has been drawn from him, and so he asks who touched him. He will not cease looking until he finds her. The disciples do not understand; she is invisible to them in the press of the crowd. But Jesus will not leave, even for the sake of the dying girl and Jairus, who wait. He will not leave until this woman is seen and heard.

Finally she emerges of her own accord. It is difficult. She is fearing and trembling, but she shows herself anyway, and falling before him, she tells him the whole truth. We do not know what she says, but we might imagine that long flow of pain, the torrent of subordinate clauses, tumbling out. Then Jesus addresses her. 'Daughter', he calls her, and in that single word she becomes no longer invisible but claimed and cherished. He tells her that it isn't his clothes that saved her, but surprisingly perhaps for a person who is dissolving with fear, it is her faith. He sends her literally 'into peace', into a state of wholeness that is greater than an end to illness and signifies what we might call a holy new beginning. Then he tells her to be healed of her scourge, so that *scourge* is the final word of her story, and perhaps in the end we are left with the memory of the pain that brought her to him, and we realize that it takes more than a moment to heal a whole life. Still, she is on her way into completeness, a person with a face, a voice and a place in the kingdom.

But we are not given time to rest in this moment, nor is Jesus. What Jairus feared most has come upon him. People from his house interrupt Jesus' words of comfort to the daughter who has been saved to tell the leader of the synagogue that for his daughter it is too late.

Jesus overhears, and here immediately we find a link between the two stories – Jairus' and the woman's – in the matter of faith. 'Do not fear, only believe', Jesus tells Jairus (5.36). The Greek verb translated *believe* has the same root as the noun for *faith* that we hear in Jesus' words to the woman because belief in Jesus isn't about taking on board a list of facts but about trusting a person, being in relationship with one who holds in himself God's love for the world.

We might be tempted to suggest that, with the command 'Do not fear, only believe', Jesus is saying that fearful people cannot be faithful, but the story of the woman makes that impossible. Two verses before this one, that fearing, trembling person – so afraid that she has only managed to approach Jesus from behind in a crowd and even then to do nothing more than touch his clothes – has been commended for her saving faith. Her faith has been effective in her and has drawn healing power from Jesus in spite of the fear that has cloaked it. So we can be sure that Jesus is not telling Jairus that if he is fearful, his daughter will die. This cannot be read as a threat because the denouement of the woman's story two verses earlier will not allow it to be. We might also turn to 9.24 for the heart-rending cry of belief and simultaneous unbelief that precedes the exorcism of another father's child. Jesus must be saying something else to Jairus, which we can discern from the woman's story and the cry of 9.24: that people of faith somehow move through fear and that faith ultimately wins. Faith trumps fear in the alternative reality of God's kingdom, and God is bigger than both, and so the story is not over.

The little girl who got up

Jesus makes his way to Jairus' house and is greeted by the commotion of grief, not the intimate grief of family and loved ones, but the racket of a world that does not know God's other way. Jesus speaks that other reality into their commotion, and they laugh at him. So he casts them out. The verb used here is the one used when Jesus casts out demons; divine hope has the power to cast out the cacophony of hopelessness, even the hopelessness of death.

Then we move with Jesus and the parents and Peter, James and John into the room of the silent, lifeless girl, and now it is her story. Jesus takes her hand and speaks to her, and we are given the words in her native tongue (as we are given Jesus' prayers to his Father from Gethsemane and Golgotha), so that the scene takes on a piercing, fragile intimacy: '*Talitha cum*,' he tells her (5.41). 'Little girl, get up!'

And she does. This girl beyond hope gets up and walks about, and she continues a life that has so far spanned the exact same number of years as the suffering of the woman at the centre of the story. Now each of them gets a new beginning with a touch and a word from the one who holds God's new thing in himself.

Both of the Greek words of resurrection are used here. And so the dying and rising of the child points to the greater new thing, the dying and rising of the saviour.

Perhaps that is why he tells them that no one must know this. Perhaps it is that if people hear about this girl, they will think that a life without death is possible. The disciples present here will certainly want to believe that. The same three will be present for the transfiguration and will not understand Jesus' words about rising from the dead (9.2–10). Then they will be present at Gethsemane but will sleep through Jesus' anguish (14.33–42) because they do not understand that to save them, he must himself first die.

So this little girl's life quietly begins again, not with trumpets or proclamation but with dinner.

Even now, after all of the healing and life and newness of Mark 5, we are not given time to celebrate. Jesus goes on to his hometown, where instead of faith he finds only un-faith, in the presence of which he can do very little. Then there is another Markan juxta-position of stories like the one in Mark 5. The disciples are sent to do their own preaching and casting out and healing, but their story is paused to tell another story of another girl, someone else's daughter, who will carry the head of John the Baptist to her mother on a platter.

But that death, that tomb, will not be the end of the story either. Jesus' disciples will return, full of the good news of their preaching and healing, and Jesus will cross the sea again, and another crowd will meet him with their needs and their hunger, and he will teach and feed and heal again, as we walk with him on our own journey towards his dying and rising and our own salvation.

Then eventually if we choose to follow beyond the end of Mark's story and to embody the gospel of Jesus in our lives, we do this not only by falling before him in brokenness, speaking our truth to his power, and trusting his life in our deathliness; we also become part of his boundary-crossing movement towards others. We speak his love into lonely, dark places, gentle words to people in pain or bondage of one kind or another (Matthew 25.34–40). We wait with voiceless sufferers until finally they find their voice, and then we listen to them. We carry Jesus' life in our fragile earthen vessels (2 Corinthians 4.7–10) as we walk alongside our neighbours through their seasons of grief. Through it all, we celebrate life and holy freedom wherever it emerges in small sparks or full-blown glory. And again and again we are amazed.

SUGGESTIONS FOR PRAYER AND EMBODIMENT

Remember a time or times in your life when you have felt called from the familiar to the unfamiliar, to otherness, to something less easy that stretches you. Note whatever comes to mind. Then select one or two memories that seem most meaningful to you now. Write down words or phrases that describe how you felt at the prospect of your crossing(s) into otherness. Then write words or phrases that describe how it felt to be there. As always, feel free to express yourself in another way, with sketches, painting or anything that works for you. Then consider in what ways that experience of the unfamiliar changed you and affected your understanding of what it means to be a person of faith in the world.

———•◆•———

Picture yourself in a very great press of people, on a city street, at a sporting event, on a subway or in another place you remember. Imagine yourself making your way towards Jesus, catching glimpses of him as you and he are jostled along in the crowd. Now reach out and touch Jesus' cloak; as you do this, you may wish to reach out and lightly brush your hand against a piece of fabric. Consider what the power of God might feel like in your body and your heart. Now imagine that Jesus stops, looking for you, waiting patiently as long as it takes as the crowd parts slightly around him, until you come forward. If you were to tell Jesus 'the whole truth' about yourself, what would it be? Tell him that now. Then listen for him as he claims you as his own and sends you into wholeness.

———•◆•———

In a reading of the story of the Gerasene, pause after 5.9, and read aloud to yourself – or ask a group member to prepare and read to the group – Psalm 88 as an expression of the person's suffering. Leave some silence after this reading in which to sit with this text, which ends without resolution. You might wish to bring to God any un-resolved questions or pain you have experienced or are experiencing, remembering that the Psalmist and the compilers of the Psalms were comfortable including this unresolved prayer in this collection and that for us, as for the Psalmists, honest expression of all of our feelings to God (including those that might feel inappropriate to us) is a gift, and God knows our hearts anyway and always holds us in love.

———•◆•———

As you are planning the reading/performance of Mark 5 for your group, consider having three sub-groups responsible for presenting the three different stories of suffering and restoration. For each story, in addition to focusing on the central figures, consider how to represent the characters around them. Feel free to enlist volunteers at the time of the performance to embody some of those parts (or even some of the central parts if you are presenting as a single reader). If you are on your own, reread the text aloud, pausing to imagine all the characters around the central characters as vividly as you can.

For 5.1–20, these might include the ones who have repeatedly tried to bind the Gerasene; the legion of demons and the swine; the swineherds who witness the event, then flee and report it (perhaps they will report it to the rest of the group); the fearful Gerasenes who see the man in his right mind and beg Jesus to leave. You might have the same group of people play the legion/swine and the Gerasenes who reject Jesus. For 5.21–24, 35–43, consider the crowd who meet Jesus; the messengers from Jairus' house; Peter, James and John; the mourners making a commotion; then the mother and the little girl. For 5.25–34, think again of the crowd pressing on Jesus and hiding the woman from view; the disciples, confused by Jesus' insistence on finding the woman in the crowd; and Jairus, waiting in silent desperation.

Experience the presentation (as performer or audience) as prayerfully and openly as you can. Then sit quietly. Remember to sit up comfortably, releasing tension from your body, as you become present to God (see 'Praying the text', p. vi). You may wish to close your eyes. What images or memories come to you as you consider what you have heard and seen? It may be that something small about the story will touch you more than a main theme or character. See what emerges. Then discuss with one or two people what you have experienced in the performance or in your reflection.

———————•◆•———————

As you study and pray Mark 5, find a gesture(s) or movement(s) that expresses some image or feeling in the stories that strikes you. You may be moved by the suffering of the Gerasene, which is expressed very violently in the passage; by Jairus on his knees before Jesus; by the woman reaching through the crowd; by Jesus turning to look for her; by the contrast between the stillness of the little girl and her walking about. Find something you can do with your body, even something very simple, to reflect that movement in the story.

In your group meeting, divide into two or more sub-groups. Share your gesture(s)/movement(s), and tell your sub-group what this expresses for you. Together put these gestures/movements in any order you like. You might add other movements that you develop together. Try doing these as a dance that you can share with the other sub-group(s). If some people are less comfortable moving in front of others, give them simpler or smaller movements with which they can feel comfortable.

If you'd like to see how simple gestures can be combined to create a dance, watch the recent reinventions by groups around the world (of all ages, all sizes, all skill levels) of a dance called 'Rosas Danst Rosas', choreographed in 1983 by Anne Teresa De Keersmaeker. Search online for Re:Rosas; then view the trailer (3 minutes 43 seconds) or the extended trailer (7 minutes 53 seconds), or watch the complete dances, and De Keersmaeker herself performing the piece, at <www.rosasdanstrosas.be>. You might also wish to view online a piece called 'Water Study', choreographed in 1928 by Doris Humphrey, in which the only sounds are made with the dancers' hands and feet. For your own dance, you could come up with sounds that you are able to make yourselves. Or you could bring an instrument if one of you plays or use a CD of music that expresses something about the passage for you. But accompaniment is not at all necessary; feel free to perform your dance in silence.

4

Following the Shepherd

Focus text	Mark 6.30–56
Reading through Mark	Mark 6.30—8.21
Poetry to pray	Isaiah 25.6–8
Supplementary passages	Psalm 23
	John 10.1–18
	Luke 15.1–7
	Ezekiel 34
	Isaiah 43.1–7
Words to take with you	Take heart, it is I; do not be afraid.

THINKING ABOUT MARK 6.30–56

The shepherd

As in the last chapter, so also here Mark begins a story, interrupts it with another, and then comes round to the first story again. The passage we are exploring now follows on from Jesus' sending of the disciples two by two in 6.7–13 to participate in his work of preaching repentance, casting out demons and healing the sick. Meanwhile in 6.14–29 we have learned of the fate of John the Baptist at the hands of the weak and fearful (and therefore especially dangerous) Herod, and that account has ended with the burial of John's body by his followers.

So we turn directly from John's disciples at his tomb to the apostles of Jesus gathering around their teacher in 6.30, and the abrupt shift casts a shadow over the scene as the narrative moves inexorably towards another execution and another tomb.

But for now these apostles are flocking around Jesus to tell him all that they have done and taught, and with them are the crowds. The word *apostles* occurs only here in Mark. The word doesn't refer to a permanent post (although it did come to be associated with a specific group in the early church), but to one who is sent for a specific task and who, for the purposes of that task, has the authority of the one who does the sending. So in that basic sense of the word, it describes each of us in the tasks large and small for which we are appointed day by day, hour by hour, minute by minute, and through which we have the authority to show God's love.

As the crowds have pressed upon Jesus so that he could not even eat (3.20), now they are pressing on his disciples. As Jesus has retreated from the crowds to a wilderness place in 1.35, so now he tells his emissaries to come away by themselves and rest a while. All of us, even Jesus, need to have our wells refilled for our own work of love.

They set off on another sea crossing, and the narrator repeats that they are going off to a wilderness place by themselves (6.31–32). The reference to the wilderness not only brings to mind Jesus' own retreat and the wilderness to which John has called the multitudes, but also evokes the wilderness of Israel's past in which God makes miraculous provision of food and water and the Sinai commandments.

The disciples are also *by themselves* with Jesus, a phrase translated elsewhere as *on their own* and *in private*. We see repeatedly in Mark that Jesus teaches the crowds and then gives additional explanation and teaching and indeed the secret of the kingdom (4.10–11, 34) to the ones who are closest to him when they are together on the way, in private homes and on sea crossings.

But in this case before they can even reach this place of retreat, the crowds have seen them going and made their way ahead of them. They have run to Jesus.

On seeing these crowds of people waiting yet again, as over and over crowds wait wherever he goes, Jesus has compassion for them (6.34). This word for *have compassion* appears again when Jesus sees the hungry crowd of 8.2 and again when the father of the boy with an unclean spirit begs Jesus in 9.22: 'if you can do anything, *have compassion* on us and help us' (ESV). And Jesus does.

The verb is based on a noun that refers to our internal organs. It is a reaction in our body – a gut-level or visceral reaction, we would say. The noun is used in Luke 1.78 to refer to the *tender mercy* of our God.

Jesus has a physical, visceral reaction of tender mercy to human need and pain in the way that each of us responds deeply and instinct-ively to vulnerability in people we love. But whereas most of us are limited in our capacity to love so deeply, Jesus has that deep compassion for each of God's children even if their need or pain might make others view them as socially unacceptable or physically unattractive or, as in this case, unwelcome in their persistence.

Jesus sees this crowd who have run around the Sea of Galilee to greet him as 'sheep without a shepherd' (6.34). This phrase evokes Old Testament images of the shepherd. David, the king whose descendant will be God's ultimate royal Messiah, is first a shepherd (1 Samuel 16.11, 18–19; 17.14–15, 20), and Moses, the prophet who is a model for the ultimate prophet to come, is tending sheep when God speaks to him from the burning bush (Exodus 3.1–2). The people of Israel are referred to as sheep needing a shepherd when they are without a good king (1 Kings 22.17) or in need of a prophet to succeed Moses (Numbers 27.15–17). When human shepherds (like Herod) fail, God is the great shepherd of his sheep (Ezekiel 34; Isaiah 40.11; Psalm 23). John 10.1–18 develops the image of Jesus as a shepherd. It is also used in one other place in Mark, where, as in John 10.11–18, it refers to Jesus' death. In Mark 14.27 on the Mount of Olives with his own, Jesus predicts that his sheep will scatter when he is struck down.

In Jesus the shepherd, not only here in 6.34 when he has compas-sion for the crowd but in all he says and does, we see God's Messiah, God's ultimate prophet, the one who acts with God's authority and love. And Jesus demonstrates what God's kingdom rule means: the compassionate prophet-king teaches, feeds, frees, heals and reaches out to his sheep (including us) precisely there where they are most in need, and most unlovely, to send them into peace. He completely embodies God's countercultural love and truth, which are so opposed to what earthly rulers comprehend that they can only kill him, and so they do.

But even that is not the end. As Jesus will in 14.28 reassure his own soon-to-be-scattered sheep (who do not understand it at the time) and us (who also often cannot take it in), God's love will go on. And God's shepherd will return to lead us into our future.

The garden party

Jesus, the shepherd, teaches his sheep by the sea.

Then the disciples start fretting. It is late, and these people are going to get hungry, and the disciples suggest that he send them away so that they can find a place to buy something for themselves to eat. But Jesus has a surprising suggestion (6.37): '*You* give them something to eat.'

The disciples see this as impossible. They cannot afford such a thing. They do not have that kind of money, and although God's agent on earth is standing before them, it does not occur to them that money is not the issue. Although they have seen Jesus at work – speaking calm to a storm, casting out unclean spirits, healing with a touch or a word, raising a little girl from the dead – still they are not able to make a connection between those past wonders and this moment of need. They think that it is all up to them.

So Jesus asks what they have and tells them to give it to him, and their scarcity becomes abundance in his hands. He makes what they have be enough for what he has told them to do.

He tells them to seat the crowd. We are given the detail of the green grass, which might remind us of the green pastures and still waters of Psalm 23 or might suggest springtime and Passover, which is when the story takes place in John 6.

He says in 6.39 that they are to be seated in *groups*, which in Greek is the repetition of the word for *symposia* (the plural of *symposium*): 'symposia symposia'. (This is a Semitic construction that we also see in 6.7 when it says 'two by two'; it says 'duo duo' in Greek.) A symposium was a dinner or drinking party, a festive company, and in Plato's *Symposium*, for example, it is also a time of philosophical discussion. We might imagine the best-ever dinner party, one that lasts into the night and is full of stimulating, restoring fellowship. We all know people with a gift for this, who manage to offer something of who they are, the best of themselves, wrapped up in the form of a lovely meal, and we might draw on that image as we consider Jesus and these dinner groups.

Then, when it says in 6.40 that the people do sit down in *groups*, a different word is used, one that literally refers to *garden plots* or *beds of plants*; so it says 'garden plots garden plots'. And this alongside the mention of the hundreds might remind us of the fruitful seeds of 4.8, 20, which produce a hundredfold. Perhaps we might see here the word that Jesus has planted in his teaching being nurtured for growth and fruitfulness by this abundant bread and fish.

There may also be a hint of a holy army being formed, like the hosts of heaven, but if so, it is as countercultural as its general-king. It is an army whose marching chants are psalms and whose only weapon is love.

As we view this garden party, this holy picnic, we might also remember that the God who speaks order into chaos in creation can speak strangers into fellowship and that the God who wishes to give us the wisdom of his word also wishes for all his children to have their physical needs met. He leads them to green pastures, and his Son invites us to pray for our daily bread. He wants to feed the hungry crowds in this wilderness as he wanted to feed the Israelites in theirs.

Here they do not even ask. They have simply sought the teacher. They have run to him. And they receive abundant grace beyond the possible.

Jesus takes, blesses, breaks and gives the bread. This will happen again at the second feeding (8.6–7), and it will also happen when the shepherd is at table with his own – his betrayer among them. There he will again take, bless, break and give (14.22–23). And so we too in our celebration at his table participate in the holiest garden party, we later sheep, sometimes running to him as they did on that Galilean meadow and sometimes scattered and needing to be sought and found and lifted into hopefulness and faith again.

In their hundreds and fifties, the five thousand men (and who knows how many women and children!) eat and are filled. There isn't a bare minimum. God's love is not a snack to tide us over until we can get something filling. There is enough divine generosity to go around and have more left over for the ones yet to come.

The shepherd on the sea

Jesus sends his disciples on another sea crossing ahead of him while he bids the crowd farewell. Then he goes up the mountain to pray. The mountain setting may remind us of his choosing of the disciples (3.13) and also point us forward to his mountaintop meeting in 9.2 with Moses and Elijah (both of whom participate in feeding miracles themselves) and to his final prayers on the Mount of Olives (14.26). It might also evoke for us again the story of Moses and the Israelites in the wilderness with Moses going up Sinai alone to meet God. But we have seen that this long-awaited 'prophet like Moses' is greater than Moses, who did not himself provide the manna, and this episode will show again the nature of this shepherd.

This crossing like the one in 4.35 begins at evening time, and then in 6.48 it is the fourth watch of the night, 3 a.m. to 6 a.m., a time when troubled souls might wish and watch for the morning (Psalm 130.6). Although they are in the middle of the sea in darkness, Jesus sees them straining at the oars against the wind. They are not perishing as in 4.38. No violent storm is mentioned. But they are struggling mightily. The word translated *straining* is used in 5.7 (in the active voice; in 6.48 it is passive) when the legion of demons beg Jesus not to *torture* them (also Revelation, where it refers to torture, as in 9.5, and to birth pains, 12.2). So the struggle against the wind, though it may not kill them, may feel wretchedly difficult all the same.

Often our struggles are that way. We may not fear for our lives; we may not even be engaged in something extraordinary. But we are pushed to, or beyond, our limits. And sometimes it may feel as if our struggle against the wind will never end, as if the morning will never come.

It is then that Jesus comes to them. Jesus, who has earlier stilled the storm and calmed the waves with a word, now walks over the water to his struggling sheep. It says that he intends to *pass them by*; this may also be an allusion to the divine at work in him. The same verb is used of God's appearances to Moses in Exodus 33.17—34.8 and to Elijah in 1 Kings 19.11–12.

But here they do not recognize him. Believing him to be a ghost rather than a saviour, they are terrified and cry out.

Jesus says, 'Take courage' (6.50). It is a single word in Greek, and it appears again in John 16.33: 'Take courage ['Be of good cheer!' in the familiar KJV]. I have overcome the world.'

Then he identifies himself with a phrase that literally means 'I am' but which is also how a person would normally say 'It is I'. And so we may read it as the latter. But under the circumstances, in which Jesus is walking on the sea, we might also hear an echo of the divine self-identification, the great *I am* of God (Deuteronomy 32.39; Exodus 3.14; Isaiah 43.10, where it appears in proximity to the beautiful images of protective divine love in 43.1–7, including God's own 'Do not be afraid').

'Do not be afraid,' Jesus says. God and angels often say this because evidently it is natural to be afraid of the most holy, and certainly awe is no bad thing; that kind of fear of the Lord is the beginning of wisdom, we are told. But there is another kind of fear that is surely not what God or Jesus or their messengers want because they say it again and again: 'Do not be afraid.' Indeed we are advised that 'perfect love casts out fear' (1 John 4.18). If we are afraid beyond the point of very reasonable awe, it is perhaps that we, like the disciples here, are not seeing him for who he is. We are not grasping the depths of compassion and strength that undergird God's steadfast love for us.

Jesus gets into the boat with them, and the wind, without a word from Jesus, ceases. Perhaps his *I am* is enough, as it is for the soldiers who fall to the ground when they hear it in John 18.6 (see also John 8.58, where the phrase incites homicidal rage in Jesus' opponents).

It says that the disciples are very exceedingly amazed (6.51). But people have been amazed before in Mark (2.12; 5.42), and it didn't mean that they understood, and the disciples here do not. Mark tells us it is because they hadn't understood about the loaves. Having failed to grasp the little thing, they do not understand this even greater manifestation of Jesus' creative power.

Their lack of understanding hearkens back to 4.12 when the outsiders did not understand, and it points us forward to the aftermath of the second feeding in 8.17–21. 'Do you still not . . . understand?' Jesus asks them. 'Are your hearts hardened?' Their hardened hearts place them in the company of Jesus' opponents in 3.5 (also 10.5), who do not wish him to heal on the Sabbath and who are so enraged when he does that they immediately begin plotting to destroy him.

Jesus' inner circle seem often to act like outsiders and enemies. But they stay close to him. They keep watching and listening, and he keeps teaching and feeding and demonstrating God's love and power until finally, after the greatest demonstration of all, these disciples do come around and become the bold proclaimers of Pentecost.

So there is hope for all of us.

On paths of righteousness

On the other side there are more crowds, as always (6.53–56). As at 5.21 and 6.34, Jesus steps off the boat and is met by all of the hopes and fears and broken hearts of the world rushing at him from all around. As before, his compassion flows even from his clothes.

Where the disciples have wanted to send people away to neighbouring villages and farms to get something to eat, Jesus himself goes to those very places so that people can reach him. He goes to the cities from which they ran to him in 6.33, and he goes to the villages and farms to which his disciples would have sent them. What's more, when all of those sick people are brought on mats to the marketplaces, he must approach each one for them to be able to touch him. He must walk slowly through the masses of people so that the fringe of his cloak is within touching distance of even the frailest, the most infirm, the least bold.

There is a gravitational pull to Jesus, which he accepts because he cares for them, all of them, insiders who do not fully understand (but try to) and outsiders who in their desperation may understand some parts of him best of all. As they are drawn to him, he is also drawn to cross geographical, social and religious boundaries to meet them. He is willing to become a political enemy of the state to the point of death when that is what it takes to do this fully.

If Jesus is in the boat with us, then no matter how many times we cross the sea at his command, what we will always find on the other side is people who need him. We are among them, his sheep. But if we want to follow him beyond the garden party and set sail across the sea, then we will be called to participate in God's love for all the rest, to share the deep compassion of Jesus for our own flock of brothers and sisters and for all the sheep on the other side of our social, religious and political boundaries of whatever kind.

He helps us do it, of course, and this passage even has some pointers.

First, it reminds us that we need to eat and rest and spend time with him apart in prayer. We have to go to the wilderness of *metanoia* and release and meet God there. It sounds so simple, but as his preachers and sowers, his emissaries of love, we will sometimes find that busy-ness overtakes us as it did those disciples, and we have to learn to hear his voice calling us away to have time with him, our teacher, healer and shepherd. We have to follow him to green pastures and still waters so that we will have the energy for the paths of righteousness. We, like the rest of the crowds, need food for body and soul.

Second, we notice in this passage that we do not have enough for what we are called to do, but he does. It isn't about what we have at all. It is about who Jesus is and what he can do with what we bring. He is the shepherd. We aren't. We participate in his love and in his abundant grace and in giving his gifts to others. But he remains the source of the gifts. He makes what we have be enough for whatever he wants us to do. It may not feel like enough. We may not feel up to it, but if it is a task he has given us to do, then he will make it enough with more to spare.

When we get it wrong, which we will, we see in this story that that doesn't mean it is over. No matter how wrong we get it or how many times, we keep showing up for duty and taking it one day at a time, learning who he is, learning who we are and what it means for each of us in our particularity to be agents of his love.

It is specifically not about how much money we have, we notice. We are called to trust God's abundance over the world's fear of scarcity, which produces a few having far too much while far too many have not enough. Part of turning around and waking up to God's alternative kingdom is learning to rest in the abundance of the shepherd-king and to base our decisions on compassion, not anxiety or fear.

That leads us to the essential lesson that we have to learn again and again. We have to learn that we are loved, deeply loved, even in the valley of the shadow of death, even in the dark, even when appearances suggest otherwise. 'Do not be afraid,' he says. And we learn to hear it, to see him there in our struggles, not a phantom, but God's love enfleshed.

SUGGESTIONS FOR PRAYER AND EMBODIMENT

Think about times when food has been a blessing to you. This might be a special meal that someone prepared for you or an ordinary one that you happen to remember lovingly or a meal you shared with someone at a restaurant (maybe something you did regularly or maybe something that happened only once); it might be a time when someone brought you a cake for your birthday or chicken soup when you were ill; or it could be an experience of the Lord's Supper that has stayed with you. Make a list of these times as you remember them. Work on this list for as long as you like, but try to go for ten minutes or more. You will likely find that some of the best surprises come to you after the memories start to emerge more slowly, so give yourself time for those to present themselves.

When you have finished the list, review it (you may prefer to wait a day to do this, but that is not necessary), see what touches you, and consider why. Is there some treasure that has emerged? Keeping in mind those memories, or your favourite one, return to the passage, and when Jesus teaches, feeds, comforts and heals, imagine the recipients of his care feeling what you felt at that moment.

Are you struggling with anything in your life like the disciples straining at the oars against an adverse wind? Consider the elements of your struggle now. Bring it to mind in its fullness. As you do this, grip this struggle very firmly in your palms. Now imagine Jesus meeting you there in this struggle and saying to you, 'Take heart, it is I; do not be afraid.' Invite him 'into the boat' with you. As you do this, relax your grip and pass this struggle over to him. Sit in silence for at least a minute and relax your body as completely as you can. Then tell Jesus anything you would like to share about your situation or simply sit in silent stillness, knowing that God is God (Psalm 46.10). Stay in prayer, with your body relaxed (releasing tension from your shoulders, hands, face), for as long as you feel comfortable and have time to do so. Then imagine Jesus returning that part of your life to you. Open your palms for it and close them very gently, and consider whether increased awareness of Jesus' presence with you might make a difference in your attitude towards your struggle or in your ability to face it.

After the second miraculous feeding, when the disciples are on the boat with Jesus worrying about not having brought enough bread, Jesus asks them if they don't remember. Read that passage again (8.14–21); then remember a time (or times) in your life when you experienced God's nearness and love. Sit with that memory, and remember it as vividly and lovingly as you can. Is there any way in which your experience of your life now might be different if you were able to embrace and trust that part of your history with God? If you are uncertain about God's present love for you, call to mind the voice of a person who loves you and imagine that voice saying to you the words of a verse about God's love; you might try Isaiah 43.1–7.

Is any part of your life so full that Jesus might be telling you to come away and rest a while? It might be full in the best possible way or in a way that is beyond your control and very difficult. Take time to be quiet on your own or in your group. If you are in a group, you could take a towel or mat to lie on if that is comfortable for you, or lie across several chairs. If you are at home, you might do this in the garden. For at least five minutes (more if possible), lie or sit comfortably still. Give yourself permission to do nothing else and to let go of any anxieties or to-do lists for now. Consider rest your holy vocation for this brief period. If you fall asleep, that is fine. After your rest, form sub-groups and brainstorm ideas, including crazy, impossible ones, for 'coming away' with Jesus from the busy-ness of life. If you are on your own, make your own list, including nonsensical notions, for holy restfulness. These can be small periods, even mere moments, for reflection or restorative activity (including vigorous activity if that is what nourishes you), alone or with someone you love. Perhaps try one in the coming fortnight.

———————

In your group, ask each person to select a Bible verse or passage that expresses God's abundant love and compassion. (If you are on your own, select your favourite verse and write, sketch, dance or express in some other way what it is about that verse that draws you.) Put all of these into a bowl and pass this around the room, letting each person pick one. In pairs or sub-groups, look these up and read them to one another. As your partner reads to you, open your heart, mind and body to God's compassion for you. Then together pick one verse or passage (it can be one you have read together or a different one) to share with the rest of the group by reading it aloud and/or by creating an image from it with your bodies, or by drawing it, colouring it, dancing it or whatever comes to mind. Give this representation of God's love to God's other 'sheep' in the room.

———————

As you prepare to read/perform Mark 6.30–56 at the opening of your group meeting, consider having food available to distribute when you reach 6.42. Leave time at that point for each person to receive a piece of food and to hold, smell and taste it (Psalm 34.8). Any food, preferably one that has a nice smell, is good. This can be the Lord's Supper if that is appropriate for your group, but this is not at all necessary; we can celebrate God's love by sharing any food or drink. Chocolate, freshly baked bread or a piece of fruit could work well for this. If you are not certain of dietary requirements in the group, you might have options available. You could even share a substantial snack at that point in the text: soup or bread with butter, jam and cheese. As you eat together, remember and celebrate that God cares for us as his sheep; that Jesus himself ate with all kinds of people (tax collectors, sinners, Pharisees, friends); that the disciples were told to take time to eat; and that God loves a feast (Isaiah 25.6–8)!

If you are going through Mark on your own, pause for a favourite food or drink at the feeding of the five thousand, or set aside a particular meal in which to celebrate God's care for you as his sheep. Or perhaps take food to someone you think might appreciate it; something as simple as a piece of chocolate or a little bag of fruit is plenty to warm anyone's heart. Include in your food package the words to a verse about food: maybe Isaiah 25.6.

5

Following the Beloved

———◆•◆———

Focus text	Mark 9.2–8
Reading through Mark	Mark 8.22—10.52
Poetry to pray	Isaiah 42.1–9
Supplementary passages	Revelation 21.1–4
	John 15.1–17
	1 Corinthians 1.18–25
	John 17.25–26
	Ephesians 5.1–2
Words to take with you	Listen to him.

———◆•◆———

THINKING ABOUT MARK 9.2–8

The Beloved on the mountaintop

Now we reach the centre of our story where we leave behind the sea and the wilderness and take our first steps with Jesus and his disciples onto the way that will lead to Jerusalem. Here at this midpoint, we find the first reference to a cross (8.34) and a second affirmation of the Son's belovedness (1.11; 9.7).

This central section of the Gospel (8.22—10.52) opens and closes with accounts of restoration of sight to the blind, which again say something about Jesus' powerful compassion, but which also, in their placement as a frame around this section, demonstrate metaphorically the struggle to see what Jesus' way means. In the first story of restoration (8.22–26), the healing comes in stages and ends in quiet retreat; when the blind man first looks, he can see people, but they look like trees walking. In a similar way, perhaps sometimes our understanding of Jesus' way comes in stages, and we need more time to take it in, as do the disciples, who in their first attempt to articulate it (8.29) get it partly right (he is indeed the Messiah) but without understanding the implications of it. In the second healing story (10.46–52), by contrast, the restoration is immediate, and faithful Bartimaeus follows Jesus on the way to Jerusalem without hesitation, leaving his old life cast off behind him like his cloak, something the disciples will be ready to do only after they see the whole truth of the dying and rising Christ.

In between those two transitional stories of moving from darkness to light, we follow Jesus and his disciples on a winding road towards understanding the mission of the Beloved and what this means for us as his followers and fellow servants of his Father.

By taking 9.2–8 as our focal point, we are choosing to view the landscape of this Gospel's central section from its highest peak. Here, as has been the case throughout Mark, those who follow closest to Jesus catch the fullest glimpse of who he is. Peter, James and John, who witnessed the raising of the little girl, climb the mountain path with Jesus now.

The passage begins with a reference to the conversation six days earlier, which has been reported immediately before (8.27—9.1). That conversation has culminated in Jesus' proclamation of the coming of God's kingdom with power (9.1). This mountaintop episode suggests right away something about what that holy power might look like.

In Jesus' moment of transfiguration (the verb used in 9.2 is the root from which we get our word *metamorphosis*), we do not find him crowned with gold and robed in ermine. Instead, his clothes become dazzling white, the colour of holiness and of martyrdom (Revelation 7.13–17). The clothes that have been a source of healing power (5.27; 6.56) and that will figure in the narrative again when he is stripped for crucifixion now shine with an unearthly luminescence.

The radiant Jesus is not enthroned but is, rather, in conversation with prophets, whose power is displayed in teaching (particularly in the case of Moses), in justice and care for the oppressed, and in acts that manifest God's feeding, healing, guiding love. This offers a stark contrast with the royal power and military might that was expected of God's Messiah.[1] Elijah and Moses stand in opposition to precisely that kind of royal authority with their prophetic power, which emerges from experiences of God's presence, including, for both of them, encounters with God on mountaintops (1 Kings 19.4–18; Exodus 24.15–18).

Both Elijah and Moses figure in Mark as important and still relevant figures from Israel's past. John the Baptist is especially associated with Elijah's return (9.13). People also speculate that Jesus himself might be Elijah or one of the prophets (6.15; 8.28); and the latter may be a reference to the hoped-for 'prophet like Moses' to whom everyone must 'listen' (Deuteronomy 18.15).

On this mountain, then, two prophetic giants of Israel's story speak with the ultimate prophet of God, who is also God's surprising Messiah and most beloved Son. In the parallel passage at Luke 9.28–36, the topic of conversation is said to be Jesus' departure (his *exodus* in Greek), which he will accomplish in Jerusalem. Mark does not say. But in placing this moment immediately after the first reference to all that is to happen in Jerusalem, he implies that at this turning point we are being given 'a foretaste of glory divine' – the strange glory that will emerge from a brutal end, which seems to promise nothing of beauty, hope or love but from which God will nonetheless bring all those things to pass.

In response to the dazzling goodness and terrifying holiness of the scene, Peter suggests they build tents (*dwellings*, NRSV) for Jesus, Moses and Elijah. This suggestion recalls the Exodus account of Moses and the Israelites in the wilderness, where the tent of meeting is overshadowed by a cloud while the glory of the Lord fills the tabernacle; the word for *tents* in Mark 9.5 is used for both *tent* and *tabernacle* in Exodus 40.34–38 (Septuagint, the Greek translation of the Old Testament in use in the first century). The proposed tents also evoke the Festival of Booths (the word *booths* is again the word translated *tents* here) during which people lived in tents in what was considered both a re-enactment of the wilderness sojourn and a looking forward to life in God's new creation (see John 7.2).

But this mountaintop moment is not meant to become static, and the glory of it cannot be contained, because Jesus does not pitch his tent away from the fragile beauty and painful struggles of humanity. It is precisely because Jesus is the sort of Messiah who attends to suffering people and suffers himself that he radiates the holiness of the God of Revelation 21.3–4, whose home (again the word for *tent*) is among human beings who need him and whose glory rests with the Israelites in their in-between place.

As Peter is suggesting festive tent-making, a cloud *overshadows* them, like the cloud of Exodus 40.34–38 and those that accompany the Son of Man (Mark 13.26; 14.62; Daniel 7.13; Revelation 1.7). In the only other New Testament appearance of that verb (Luke 1.35), Gabriel tells Mary that she is to be *overshadowed* by the Holy Spirit. God's presence descends and does new, impossible things, and here, as in Mary's story, the heavenly voice tells us that the newness comes wrapped in a Son.

The baptismal voice of 1.11 claims Jesus again. This time the voice speaks not to Jesus but directly to the disciples and to us: 'This is my Son, the Beloved.' Then a command: 'Listen to him!'

The first line of the Gospel proclaims that Jesus is the Son of God. The unclean spirits shout it (1.24; 3.11; 5.7). At what might seem Jesus' most ungodly moment, a stranger at the foot of the cross affirms it (15.39). But other than in the two parental declarations of love (1.11; 9.7), the only place where the phrase *beloved son*, or even the word *beloved*, appears in Mark is in the parable of the vineyard in 12.1–12, which highlights the connection between Jesus' particular belovedness and the rejection, death and resurrection that await him, along with the cross that he says in 8.34–39 (which we'll discuss in Chapter 6) may await his followers.

So we move forward from the mountaintop for a moment to visit that vineyard now.

The beloved son and the violent vinegrowers (12.1–12)

Jesus addresses the parable of the vineyard to the religious authorities in Jerusalem, who are looking for an opportunity to kill him after his display at the temple in 11.15–18 (and who have been condemned metaphorically in the framing image of the fruitless fig tree, 11.12–13, 20). They have lost a battle of wits with him in 11.33, and now he continues that conversation, beginning in 12.1 with a cluster of allusions to the vineyard of Isaiah 5.1–7, which brings immediately into view God's relationship with Israel and its leaders.

Jesus' parable tells the story of a distant owner and the leasing of the vineyard to tenants. The word translated *tenants* (NRSV) is the word for *farmer* or *vinedresser* or, as in John 15.1, *vinegrower*. There, in John, the vinegrower is God himself. Here, in Mark, the lord of the vineyard (12.9, *owner,* NRSV) is linked with the Lord of the Psalm (12.11). He leaves the vineyard in the care of these vinegrower-tenants, so that it becomes their story too, as Jesus' hostile audience realizes.

The faithful slaves of 12.2–5 are generally understood to represent the prophets who have preceded Jesus, including John the Baptist, whose beheading might be evoked by the wound to the head of the second slave. We might also see here a reference to the faithful slaves who follow Jesus and await the return of the master (13.34–37), the ones (including us) who are told in 8.34–35 and 13.9–13 that following him means taking on board the risk of suffering for the sake of God's good news.

The treatment of the slave-emissaries in the vineyard grows progressively worse until finally there is but one left to send, the beloved son. So the lord of the vineyard sends his son, and the vinegrower-tenants, seeing a chance to take over the vineyard, seize the son, kill him and cast him out.

'What then will the [lord] of the vineyard do?' asks Jesus (12.9). He will come and destroy the tenants and give the vineyard to others and the beloved son will be vindicated. This vindication is expressed by a citation of Psalm 118.22–23. The stone the builders rejected (the word used of Jesus' rejection in 8.31) has become the chief cornerstone. The Lord will achieve this amazing reversal of circumstances.

The parable tells the story of the beloved Jesus in a nutshell. If we listen to Jesus, as the voice from the cloud commands, that is what we hear again and again. To be God's Beloved means to be sent down from the shining glory of the mountaintop into a suffering world to bring God near. Then, because the world as it is cannot accommodate God's alternative kingdom way in all its glorious fullness and because God's Son comes in love and not with military might, it means a cross.

But after three days, the amazing, utterly surprising reversal that only the Lord could achieve: the Beloved will be raised.

Listening to the Beloved

As we saw at Jesus' baptism, where the divine 'I love you' was followed immediately by Jesus' being cast out into the wilderness to face Satan, so also here, following Jesus' shining moment of transfiguration, we find that being God's beloved Child (the word *beloved* here can also have the connotation of *only* or *favourite*) does not mean a life of ease, a life of ceaseless glory on a mountaintop or a life of military success and royal privilege. Rather, it means that Jesus is uniquely equipped to bring God's love and holy power near, both in the cosmic battle with Satan (played out in miniature with Jesus' casting out of unclean spirits, 3.23–27) and in the smaller struggles of the suffering, grieving, hungry people to whom Jesus chooses to be present. And so when the disciples turn around with the voice of heavenly love and the command to listen ringing in their ears, the splendour is gone, and they find Jesus alone, ready to continue on his way to Jerusalem and, in the first instance, to descend to the crowds again and to the cries of another unclean spirit.

Jesus' first words to these disciples after they have been told to listen to him include references to his rising from the dead (9.9) and to his suffering (9.12), both of which have figured in his teaching of 8.31—9.1, immediately preceding the account of his mountaintop metamorphosis.

In 8.31, after ordering the disciples to tell no one that he is the Messiah, he explains precisely what this will mean. He tells them all of this again, in more or less detail, at 9.31 and 10.33–34. It is the refrain that punctuates this section of the Gospel. In each case the refrain is followed by what we might call Variations on a Theme of Misunderstanding, as the disciples demonstrate confusion both about Jesus' mission and about its implications for them.

So we listen to the Beloved now, and we listen to the misunderstandings of his followers and bring our own confusion to these conversations on the way.

We step back six days from the mountaintop to 8.27—9.1. We listen as Jesus makes the first prediction of his dying and rising. Then we overhear as Peter rebukes him. Jesus, who has himself rebuked unclean spirits (1.25) and unruly wind (4.39), turns and looks not just at the wayward pupil Peter, but at all the disciples, suggesting that all (and surely we as well sometimes) are implicated in what follows. Addressing Peter as Satan, so that this becomes not so unlike the earlier rebukes of demonic forces, Jesus rebukes Peter, whose mind is set on human things, not God's.

This verb for *setting one's mind* on something occurs frequently in the New Testament letters (for example, Philippians 2.5; Colossians 3.2), where we hear that how we think shapes who we are and what we do (see also Romans 12.2, where the verb *transfigure* is used of the *transforming* of our minds so that we can do God's good and perfect will). Jesus also tells Peter to 'get behind' him, which could be putting him physically in his place as a disciple; this suggests that the orientation we choose through our actions may also affect our ability to set our minds on the things of God. In other words, we find both that where we choose to focus our minds shapes our actions and also that sometimes, when our mind is straying, setting our feet, hands and bodies in the right direction – acting like followers of God's Beloved – reorientates our minds.

After Jesus' second passion-resurrection prediction (9.31), the ungodly mindset of misunderstanding continues with the disciples arguing who among them is the greatest. Then after the third full prediction (10.33–34), James and John ask to be seated at places of honour beside Jesus in his glory, not realizing that bandits will soon be at his right and his left in death; and the others respond in anger – perhaps because James and John got there first! In each case the disciples demonstrate what setting our minds on human things might look like, and Jesus turns their attention back to the upside-down values and aspirations of God's kingdom. They continue to cling to the idea that we have a Messiah who chooses privilege for himself and so will grant privilege to his followers, by association. But that is not what being God's beloved favourite looks like.

When the disciples repeatedly misunderstand, they are still in the middle of this story; they are not yet the formidable preachers of

Pentecost we know they will become. At this point in their story they share the normal expectation of their time that God's Messiah-king will triumph on a human plain over a flesh-and-blood enemy. But God's plan is for victory on a cosmic plain, which can be won only by the one with greater love. That is God's weapon and creative power. So the one who knows that love best of all, the Beloved himself, is best equipped to take it to the end on a cross and to embody the dazzling resurrection-reversal that God will enact.

For many of us, even though we do know the whole story, it can be difficult to hold in our minds at the same time the cross and resurrection of Jesus. Some of us find it easier to grasp the message of the cross than the radiance of the resurrection because evil and suffering are present the world over. And, of course, the cross lies within the domain of the historian; its stark reality is not a matter of faith. God's goodness can be more difficult to grasp.

There are also surely some of us who embrace the cross without taking in the horror of it because we are so accustomed to hearing about it since childhood – when the obscene brutality had to be censored – that it has become domesticated, and we no longer see it as the dreadful torture that it was. When Peter rebukes Jesus, the notion of Jesus' violent death has not become domesticated for him, and so we can perhaps have sympathy for him in his certainty that such a way could not be God's.

On the other hand, others of us find it easier to grasp the resurrection. We have known God's love intimately, felt God's life coursing through and around us in ways so beautiful that the memory is beyond words. And perhaps we, like Peter, would like to enclose the shining Jesus in a lovely tent and hold him safe on the mountain.

But if this is our good news, then all of it is our good news, and the Beloved, to whom we are commanded to listen, is telling the truth about God's presence in all of it. It is all part of God's mysterious love story with the world.

If we do not maintain the tension between the cross and the resurrection, we struggle to grasp the significance of either.[2] Jesus must die because he is the complete embodiment of a way that transcends, and therefore threatens, all notions of authority beyond God's own authority. He must die for that reason and also because if he does not take the way of vulnerable humanity to its highest and lowest point, then he cannot be in himself the way for all of us, at our most golden and our darkest points. He cannot demonstrate God's steadfast love from which nothing can separate us, not even death, unless he dies. And he must rise for the same reasons: because he is a complete embodiment of God's way, which is the way of life, and because in rising he lifts us in our vulnerable humanity into God's eternal love.

When Jesus tells Peter, James and John to keep the experience of the transfiguration to themselves, it may be because he knows that they, and any who hear of it, will be tempted to cling to an idea that the glory is possible without the suffering and death he insists is to come. But it isn't. The cross and the glory are, paradoxically, one.

And so the Son of Man will suffer; Jesus says it again as they descend the mountain (9.12). Not only that, but Elijah, the one who is to come first, has come (by implication, in the person of John the Baptist), and they have done to him what they will do to Jesus. Many faithful slaves have died as emissaries of the lord of the vineyard because people struggle to accept the idea of submitting to God's reign, which undermines their grasp on things and turns everything upside down; and when powerful people are cornered, even by God's great love, they tend to resort to violence.

If we listen to Jesus as faithfully as we can and still do not get it, still cannot conceive of the strange glory of the cross, that should not surprise us too much. We know that God's perspective on the cross is beyond human understanding. As Paul puts it (1 Corinthians 1.22–25), the idea of a crucified Christ is foolishness and a stumbling block. That word for *stumbling block* is the nominal form of the verb for *falling away* in Mark 4.17, for *make to stumble* in 9.42–47 and for *become deserters* in 14.27. In other words, that sort of falling away and stumbling and desertion is the effect one would expect the idea of a crucified saviour to have on people. But, Paul continues, seen through the eyes of faith, it is the power of God and the wisdom of God (Isaiah 55.8–9).

We people of faith do not celebrate Easter before standing faithfully at the cross and then moving faithfully to the stone-closed tomb. We might voice a lament at the suffering and dying of the Beloved, but that is proper for people whose sacred texts include the Psalms.

And even through our faithful lament, we embody the good news that God is at work in all of it because Jesus, to whom we have been commanded to listen, told us so, and we, like God, love him.

Down the mountain

Mark is a good book for people in the messy middle of life. It shows us the glory from the start and lets us glimpse the radiance of the mountaintop along the way, but it will not let us dwell there without also leading us through the strange wilderness of the cross. It will not let us be near Jesus and overlook the suffering crowds who run to him at every turn. It will not let us celebrate the Holy Spirit without hearing the cries of the unclean spirits, drawn painfully and inexorably to the one who will destroy them and free the oppressed person whose body and soul they torment. Mark forces us to see that it is not in glorious isolation but in these hard places that God especially chooses to dwell. And so Jesus is perhaps most likely to seek us out not when we are at our most luminescent but when we are at our point of greatest need.

Peter is not rebuked for his confusion on the mountaintop, and maybe that is because it is natural to wish to harness our experience of the heights of holiness. But even if they are fleeting or only out of the corner of our eye or from behind, like Moses' view of God passing as he hides in the cleft of the rock (Exodus 33.18–23), glimpses of holiness stay with us. They work their way into our bones and become a source of courage long after we have left the mountaintop.

And if we may not cling exclusively to the glory, we must also not allow ourselves to miss it. Listening to him means hearing the whole story. Although the disciples cannot have a festival with Elijah and Moses, they do get to see them with Jesus in his radiance. And although Jesus does direct their attention again to the suffering that the Son of Man must face (9.12–13), it is only after promising them again that he will also rise (9.9).

We walk down the mountains of our lives in the confidence that even if we are heading for the valley of the shadow of death, God's best Beloved goes ahead of us into the need, lostness and heartache of the world. If we wish to see what holy belovedness looks like, we look at him and his teaching, healing, feeding, boundary-crossing compassion. This one who is stronger than Satan shows us that being God's person means taking the way of love no matter where it leads and that we also are destined for a love that will guide everything else we do – we who are also beloved (Ephesians 5.1–2), no longer only slaves but also friends (John 15.15), his brothers and sisters even (Romans 8.14–17), we whom nothing, not our heights nor our depths, not even a cross, can separate from God's love.

SUGGESTIONS FOR PRAYER AND EMBODIMENT

Bring to mind a mountaintop or hilltop you know. Now imagine yourself ascending it with Jesus and two of his disciples or two people you know. As you reach the summit, consider how Jesus might look in his radiant metamorphosis; then form an image in your mind of Moses and Elijah joining him there in conversation. What might they look like? Picture the scene as vividly as you can. Someone suggests building tents – is that you or someone else? Suddenly the cloud overshadows you. What does it look like – white or dark? And you hear the voice. What does the voice sound like? Is it female or male? Is it the voice of an elderly person, a young person, a person of indeterminate age? Does the command to listen sound gentle and encouraging or awe-inspiring and thunderous? Now imagine the cloud gone and Jesus standing there alone, looking like you and me, a human being whose heart can soar or break, whose body can tire, whose feet can get dusty, whose hands can hold the hands of another.

At this moment, what does it mean to you that Jesus is God's Beloved? Does listening to what he says in the immediately surrounding passages and seeing him here affect your understanding of what it means for God to love you?

Consider the command to 'Listen to him' as you go through the next week. Open the door of your mind to him as you go about your daily activities, or spend time listening in silence or through the 'Poetry to pray' or a 'Supplementary passage'. In the course of the week, or once at the end, write or create something to express your response to your time of listening, or revisit the mountaintop with Jesus and create a response to that.

———————

Make a list of 'mountaintop' experiences in your life, moments of unusual beauty or goodness. The most interesting things are some-times in the recesses of our minds, so you may need time to move through things on top before you reach them. If you seem to slow down, sit a little longer and see what else comes.

As you reflect on your list, does it teach you anything about your-self and God's call of love in your life? Is there a treasure here that you might take with you now about the circumstances, activities or people that help you open up spaces in yourself where you feel closest to the glory of God? Ask God to speak to you through these memories.

———————

In your group or on your own, as you begin your usual time for becoming present to God in silence, those who are able might try walking through their prayer. You could do this outside – maybe even on a hillside – where you might notice the give of the earth, the cool of the breeze or the warmth of the sun against your skin. You might hear the sounds of animals, the wind in the trees, your footfall (maybe the crunch of snow or leaves under your feet), the hum of cars in the distance, birdsong. If you are inside, notice the sensation of your feet moving across the floor. Attend to the feel of the air; notice whether it is still or moving, warm or cool. Become aware of the sounds in the room and any that are audible from outside.

Now imagine yourself following Jesus up the mountain. The 'Focus text' (9.2–8) begins with the phrase 'Six days later'. Cast your mind back to Mark's account in 8.27—9.1 of what the disciples have experienced six days before. A member of the group could read those verses while others walk, or you could read them to yourself if you are alone. Does anything strike you? Does any word or phrase linger in your mind? Is there anything you would like to say to Jesus about the passage as you walk with him? Speak to Jesus, or walk in silence with him.

After your time of walking meditation, sit quietly and listen to the presentation of 9.2–8, or read it to yourself if you are praying on your own.

———◆·◆·◆———

If anyone in the group speaks another language or if several people do, try reading 9.2–8 aloud in other languages; you should be able to find the text online. Help people understand what is happening through intonation, facial expressions and hand movements, or perhaps recruit one or more members of the group who are comfortable with movement to move through the story while you speak it. (If you are on your own, you might ask a bilingual friend, perhaps someone from another country, to read the text to you; you could do this over the phone.) Do you hear or experience anything new when the passage is spoken in another language? Does the idea of listening to Jesus as something beyond language appeal to you?

———◆·◆·◆———

Invite one person or a series of people to communicate the story of the transfiguration from Peter's perspective – in their own words, with a combination of words and movement or just with movements. You could imagine Peter speaking immediately after the transfiguration. Or you could imagine Peter looking back on this time from a post-resurrection or post-Pentecost perspective. (If you are working on your own, you could do this for yourself or discuss your thoughts with a friend.) Allow time to prepare so that you can consider how Peter might reflect on his mountaintop experience based on what has happened to him six days earlier (8.27—9.1); you might even wish to begin there as you tell the story.

6

Following the Lover

Focus text	Mark 12.28–34
Reading through Mark	Mark 11—13
Poetry to pray	Song of Songs 8.6–7
Supplementary passages	Luke 10.25–37
	Matthew 5.43–48
	John 13.1–5, 34–38
	1 John 4.7–21
	Luke 12.22–34
Words to take with you	You shall love.

THINKING ABOUT MARK 12.28–34

Love has the last word

Now we arrive in Jerusalem, where Jesus must face the murderous keepers of the vineyard, who have from the start opposed his proclamation and embodiment of God's alternative kingdom way.

As God's parental love stood at the peak of the Gospel's central section, love can also be said to stand at the centre of these prepassion chapters. Here love gets the last word before the authorities resort to violence.

In what has been the last straw, Jesus has openly condemned (11.17), and physically disrupted (11.15–16), the economically exploitative practices of the temple, 'a den of robbers' where the poor give all they have (12.41–44) for a system that benefits the powerful, privileged and corrupt (12.38–40). That confrontation has issued in a final determination among the religious elite to kill him. The conflict has played out in the meantime in a series of verbal skirmishes in the temple: first, a discussion of Jesus' authority initiated by the chief priests, scribes and elders, to which Jesus has responded with the parable of the vineyard; then an attempt by some Pharisees and Herodians to test him (the word for *putting to the test* in 12.15 is used of Satan in 1.13); and finally an almost comical exchange with some Sadducees, which has concluded with Jesus telling them that they understand neither the Scriptures nor the power of God, and are greatly in error.

It is directly on the heels of this extended verbal romp through the religious power structure that Jesus is approached by a scribe, a representative of a group who have opposed Jesus from the Gospel's earliest chapters (2.6–7, 16; 3.22) and who are among the ones Jesus has said will be responsible for his suffering and death (8.31; 10.33). The scribes and chief priests have already begun looking for an opportunity to kill him (11.18); and they will mock him as he suffers on the cross (15.31). Even beyond their opposition to Jesus, the scribes are criticized by the crowds for the lack of authority in their teaching (1.22), are said to be guilty of the only unforgivable sin (3.29–30), and will soon be condemned by Jesus for their hypocrisy and exploitation of the poor (12.38–40).

But this scribe surprises us. He hears and sees rightly – important things to do in Mark. And he asks Jesus a legitimate question, which elicits the teaching that undergirds all the rest (12.28): 'Which commandment is the first of all?'

To love God

Jesus responds with a twofold answer (12.29–31). The first half is drawn from Deuteronomy 6.4–9, called the *Shema*, for the Hebrew word *hear*, with which the passage opens: 'Hear, O Israel: the Lord our God, the Lord is one.' Mark alone includes this verse in the love commandment; Luke and Matthew begin with 6.5.

We read in James 2.19 concerning God's oneness that 'even the demons believe – and shudder', which might remind us of all the crying, fearful demons in Mark, who recognize that the one God is powerfully present in the Son. Jesus' inclusion of the phrase picks up on the ongoing conversation in Mark about who Jesus is and the source of his power, which has been the question raised by the authorities in the conversation of 11.28 and which Jesus will address implicitly in the teaching of 12.35–37, where he suggests that if the Messiah is David's Son, he certainly isn't only that. But in case there were any doubt, Jesus affirms the monotheistic basis of Judaism here. As in John, where Jesus affirms explicitly and repeatedly that the Father and Son are one, so also here in Mark the basis for that relationship of oneness and the inclusion of others in it will be love.

After this statement about the one and only God of Israel, Jesus says how we are to relate to that one Lord: 'you shall love the Lord your God with all your heart, and with all your soul, and with all your mind, and with all your strength.'

The *Shema* includes only the heart, soul and might (the word for *might* in the Septuagint is the one we find used in Mark 5.30, for example, to refer to Jesus' *power*). However, the word used for *mind* in Mark 12.30 can also translate the Hebrew word for *heart*, which is to say that all of these – heart, soul, mind, strength/might – are, in a sense, of a piece. It is not a question of four isolated aspects of ourselves as if we might consider engaging one but not the others. The word for *soul* is elsewhere translated *life*, and after one speaks of loving with one's whole life, there can be little more to add! But every possible expression of that is included here to emphasize that there is to be no dimension of ourselves, no part of our lives, in which we do not put this radical demand first.

Attending to each element of the command enriches our understanding of what it means to love in this comprehensive way.

The understanding of the heart that we find here is not a touchy-feely greeting-card concept. We see this especially when we notice problems of the heart in Mark. When the heart is hardened: the scribes do not recognize the power of the Son of Man to forgive sins (2.6–8); the Pharisees and Herodians are more interested in religious regulations than in the life-giving healing of a man with a withered hand, and they wish to destroy Jesus for the sake of their principle (3.5–6); and Jesus' own inner circle cannot understand the one to whom they have committed their very lives (6.52; 8.17). The heart is also the source of defilement and evil intentions (7.21–23). And so, when we love with all our heart, it is a matter not simply of feelings but of perception and intent. In Luke we find people pondering, wondering, reasoning and thinking in their hearts. The heart set on God has a wisdom beyond what even the most reasonable among us is able to think.[1]

We will discuss the soul/life of love later in this chapter. It is enough to say here that it is this soul/life that the Son of Man will give as a ransom for many (10.45), and it is this that the shepherd of John 10.11–18 will lay down and take up again out of love for the sheep and the Father. And yet we are not to worry about our own soul/life because it is entirely in God's care; we are invited to consider the lilies and ravens to understand what this means (Luke 12.22–34).

A number of words are used for *mind* in the New Testament. The one used here appears also in the Magnificat when God scatters the proud in the *imagination* of their hearts (Luke 1.51). It appears in Hebrews 8.10 in a citation of Jeremiah 31.31–34 where it sits in parallel with the heart, as God puts his laws in people's minds and writes them on their hearts. In 1 Peter 1.13 we are directed, literally, to 'gird up the loins of [our] minds' or, as the NRSV puts it, 'prepare [our] minds for action'. Our mind, or imagination, is an active place that moves us. It is where we are transformed in the act of repentance/ *metanoia*. It is the place where we direct ourselves towards God and in which God works to reach us. To love with it is to engage our imagination beautifully (Philippians 4.8) and gird up the loins of our thoughts determinedly in the direction of God.

Strength here might suggest the engagement of our bodies in the work of love, and it is no doubt true that if we are to engage our whole self, that includes our physical self. But to define love's strength in this way is problematic for two reasons. In the first place, we are of a piece; our bodies do not function independently of our minds and hearts. In addition, to limit strength to physical strength is to confuse it with brute force and to miss Mark's larger portrait of what it means to be strong. The model for strength in Mark is Jesus himself, the one stronger than the wilderness prophet John (1.7). He is strong enough to bind the strong man Satan (3.27). His strength is greater than the immense force of a legion of demons who are able to wrench chains apart and break fetters in pieces (5.4). In other words, strength in Mark is something beyond physical strength and in the realm of the spiritual. It is the Holy Spirit that empowers us with this kind of strength to fight God's battle of love for the world's heart.

By saying it in every possible way, both the *Shema* and the variant of it cited by Jesus make clear the level of absolute, fundamental, complete commitment behind this love of God. And because for Jesus it must emerge organically from this first commandment, he inextricably links that commitment to a wholehearted love of neighbour.

To love our neighbour

When we have directed all of ourselves towards God, God then turns the attention of our heart, soul, mind and strength in the direction of our neighbours and says, 'Now love them too.'

The love under discussion here is obviously not merely a feeling. Feelings come and go – affected, as we all know, by blood sugar, hormones, exercise, lack of sleep, any chemicals we put into our bodies (including caffeine and alcohol), illness, bereavement and a host of factors beyond our control. If love were just a feeling, it could hardly be commanded. Real love, while it certainly moves in and from the deepest part of ourselves, is a choice, which means it is a matter of will, thoughtfulness and action.

We are often not instinctively loving. We are often instinctively fearful and, therefore, selfish, and we have to choose to move beyond, through and around that to love. Of course, it is easier to make the choice to love – and it is more instinctive to us and something we are more likely to feel – if circumstances are in our favour. But even if they are not, we can choose to take this 'more excellent way' above all others (1 Corinthians 12.31—13.13).

Still, choosing to love our neighbours can be a challenge. It is potentially much harder than the command to turn ourselves absolutely towards God. But it is not optional. That is perhaps why this commandment, drawn from Leviticus 19.18, appears repeatedly in Scripture. In addition to offering a full portrait of love to the Corinthians, Paul repeats the command to love your neighbour in Romans 13.8–10 and Galatians 5.13–15. It appears in James 2.8 and 1 John

4.7–21. It is in all of the Gospels in one form or another: in Luke 10.25–37 with the parable of the neighbour we would least expect; in Luke 6.27–36 and Matthew 5.43–48 with the command to love our enemies; in John 13.34–35 with the command to love one another, which in that context refers to members of the community of Jesus' followers, and this is no small matter either – as we all know, relationships within and between churches can be shockingly unloving.

Mark does not explore the identity of our neighbour, but we can presume from the model of Jesus' behaviour in Mark and his compassion for the least socially appealing and the most socially acceptable, for the voiceless and the privileged, that our neighbours include everyone and especially those who most need compassion and help and who are least likely to get it.

We love them. We love God. These together are our highest aim.

The scribe agrees (12.32–33). He affirms and elaborates on Jesus' answer. He begins with the oneness of God, which means that we hear it twice in Mark; the scribe underscores it by adding that 'besides him there is no other' (Isaiah 45.18–23). Then the scribe draws a comparison between love and 'all whole burnt-offerings and sacrifices'. Religious ritual is only meaningful when our first commitment to love is met (Hosea 6.6). In the context of Jesus' stay in Jerusalem, where this appears in the narrative, we see what it looks like when church and religion go awry and become systems of oppression, complicit in evil, as Jesus has already made clear with the parable of the vineyard and his actions in the temple. But this isn't just about them – it rarely is! It is always true that being religious and doing church are secondary and only meaningful if love for God and neighbour is primary; their significance derives from love, and without love, they are nothing or worse than nothing.

Jesus' last words to this scribe are the last words he addresses to any of his opponents before they arrest and kill him: 'You are not far from the kingdom of God.' It is perhaps a hopeful sign that even one of those who have opposed him from the start can get it right (can speak intelligently, as Jesus observes). It may also suggest that in Jesus, God's kingdom draws near to everyone, and those who draw near to Jesus for any purpose are within touching distance of it (Luke 17.20–21).

That it is to an enemy that Jesus reveals the hermeneutical key to understanding all that he has done and taught is perhaps appropriate. It is in itself an act of boundary-crossing love.

And the opponents are stymied. They do not dare to ask him any more questions. The next time anyone *dares* to do something (or *goes boldly* as the NRSV puts it in 15.43), it will be another from among their ranks, Joseph of Arimathea, who, like the scribe, steps away from the pack of Jesus' enemies in his quest for the kingdom way. He will dare to ask Pilate for Jesus' body.

Loving as he loves

Whom Jesus loves (10.17–31)

There is only one other use of the word *love* in Mark. In 10.17 as Jesus is setting out 'on the way', a man runs to him and asks him how to inherit eternal life. Jesus is said to love him (10.21) as he tells him that the one thing he lacks is to sell his possessions and give the money to the poor, to embody love of neighbour as completely as he has embodied love for God in a lifetime of obedient piety. He must change his priorities dramatically in order to be freed for the enduring fullness of life he seeks.

By implication, it is because we are loved that we are called to embody love in extraordinary ways – to love God and neighbour in the way that Jesus does, absolutely and to the end and beyond the end into God's forever. Doing this, making this fundamental choice, frees us to follow Jesus and gives us the proper treasure for life in the kingdom of God.

The man goes away grieving.

Even for those of us who have followed the commandments from our youth and actively sought, even run to, the very person who can guide us into fullness of life, choosing God's way wholeheartedly and completely will sometimes be impossible.

The disciples are appalled when Jesus tells them that a person could forfeit fellowship with Jesus and passage through the kingdom gates over wealth, and they ask him who then can be saved, the implication being that if a candidate as good as this man can't get in, where's the hope for the rest? But it turns out that the case of the man is not hopeless. Jesus tells the disciples that, while it may sometimes be impossible for mortals to face successfully these ultimate challenges that emerge when we choose God's way, it is not impossible for God. For God all things are possible. So God makes a way where there is none in us.

What follows on that exchange with the man who cannot let go is a discussion with Peter about all that he and Jesus' other closest followers have given up for the sake of Jesus and his good news (10.29): house, brothers, sisters, mother, father, children and fields. We have seen the fishermen leave behind their boats and nets to follow Jesus, and in the case of James and John their father, and we have watched Levi walk away from his tax booth. They have demonstrated the total commitment that Jesus asks of those who run to him, like this one he is specifically said to love. Now Jesus tells them that they will get all of it back. He does not say how or in what form; it may be that the family of people 'on the way' become brothers, sisters and mothers not only to Jesus (3.33–35) but also to one another. This comes with persecution (10.31; 13.9–13) and happens in the context of the upside-down values of God's kingdom, where people we'd expect to be first, like the rich man whom Jesus loves, are not. But it also comes with eternal life, the very thing the man ran to Jesus to find.

Love and our life (8.34–38)

After the first passion-resurrection prediction, Jesus lays out for his disciples and for the crowd the implications of his mission for those who wish to follow him. If we wish to do this, he says in 8.34–38, then we are to deny ourselves, take up our cross and follow. Then Jesus talks about what this means in accounting terms, in terms of what we forfeit and what we gain – counting the cost of discipleship, we might say (Luke 14.25–33). We give up what seems to be our life only to find that in the economy of the kingdom of God we have saved it.

There, as in the love commandment, our whole soul is in play. The word for *life* in 8.35–37 is the Greek word *psyche*, translated *soul* in 12.30 – to love with our whole soul. In both cases, in the choice to follow Jesus as he expresses it in 8.34–38 and in the choice to love

God and neighbour as Jesus commands in 12.29–31, we are making a radical choice to place our whole soul, our very life, on the line.

Read in the context of what it means to love and of how Jesus embodies love in Mark, we can see that this self-denial and taking up of the cross cannot be references to suffering generally. Throughout Mark we have seen Jesus' compassion for people enduring all kinds of suffering, hunger and social isolation and his willingness to cross boundaries – geographic, social and religious – to help them. He does not see their suffering as a necessary taking up of their cross; he sees it as something from which they should be freed, even when doing that threatens his own life. The first mention of plans by religious and political authorities to kill Jesus is prompted by a healing on the Sabbath (3.6).

When we are called to take up our cross and follow him, it is into that sort of fearless, boundary-crossing, holy work of the shepherd, even when it offends the status quo and even when that status quo has the power to harm us – to put the cross-beam of the executioner on our backs as would be the case in a Roman crucifixion. The reference to the cross is specifically to that possibility of losing our lives as enemies of the powerful. With even that possibility in view, we are to set our minds on God's way and live as citizens of his kingdom, where the last are first, the rich are in peril, service to the smallest and humblest is valued over recognition by society's greatest, and love is the first commandment.

To deny ourselves is to refuse to deny, or be ashamed of (8.38), Jesus and his strange good news of a strength that undermines and frees everything that isn't love. It is to refuse to deny him even when claiming his way puts our life on the line (13.9–13). The only other uses of the word *deny* in Mark occur in the account of Peter's denial of Jesus (14.30–31, 66–72). Peter says he will die rather than deny Jesus (14.31; in John 13.37 he says he will lay down his *psyche*), but, within hours, he has failed dramatically. What makes Peter a particularly good example of denial is that we know, as readers and hearers of Mark have always known, that this is not the end of his story; it isn't even the end of his story in Mark (16.7). If fear or pride causes us to stumble, it isn't the end of our story either. God calls us back to his life-giving love, and we return to his excellent kingdom way.

Jesus' followers are not being told to choose death. We are being told to choose life, and not just any life but the best, most love-filled, most enduring life. It is a choice of God's life over any other (Deuteronomy 30.15–20). Although it may sometimes be the ultimate challenge, it is also beautiful and freeing to lessen our grip on whatever stands between us and that life – whatever damages our heart, soul, mind and strength and whatever offers a false sense of security, including things that may look attractive to us or people around us. Surely most of us recognize (even if we are unable to act on it sometimes) that clinging to and striving after things that are not God's best way is fundamentally enervating and pointless, and what Jesus is inviting his followers to do is merely the largest, most complete version of taking that best way of love.

Claiming Jesus and denying what appears to be our self-interest may actually align us against powerful people in our lives. But for many of us the most difficult challenge we face may be, as it was for the rich man of 10.22–23, the rejection of our own religious, political and social ideals, things we have been taught and have believed, which can be powerful deterrents and very hard to see past. The challenge may be to give up something that figures into our sense of who we are and walk away from deeply internalized social scripts about what it means to be secure, attractive and successful.

After Paul writes in Philippians 3.4–14 about his superb CV (his 'reason to be confident in the flesh', which does not refer to our bodies but is another way of describing our susceptibility to things that might lure us away from Jesus' best way), he says that he has come to see it all as rubbish in light of 'the surpassing value of knowing Christ Jesus'. He has again and again walked straight into danger; he provides a catalogue of all he has suffered in his ministry in 2 Corinthians 11.24–28. Even as he writes to the Philippians, he is in prison. And yet 'forgetting what lies behind and straining forward to what lies ahead [he presses] on towards the goal for the prize of the heavenly call of God in Christ Jesus' (Philippians 3.13–14). That is how it feels to do what Jesus invites in Mark 8.34–38 and commands in 12.29–31. It feels like forgetting, denying and leaving behind us all of our past successes and failures and walking straight through our pride and our fear into God's radical love.

Even if our wholehearted commitment of our life to love of God and neighbour never amounts to imprisonment or execution or loss of job, family and friends (13.9–13; 10.28–30), it will involve a choice that is fundamental to who we are or what we have been taught to be or how we function in the world. But we will find that the way that looks like loss is gain, and casting off what looks like treasure frees us for something that does not weigh us down but lifts us up. We will see that by risking everything in our own embodiment of divine love, paradoxically, we save our lives.

SUGGESTIONS FOR PRAYER AND EMBODIMENT

Remember times when you have felt loved. This could be something a parent or another loving person did for you regularly as a child. It could be something a stranger said or did for you once as an adult, someone whose name you never knew and whose face you cannot remember. It could be an experience of a place where you had the sense that everything around you loved you. Write down whatever comes to you. For the first five minutes, you are likely to remember people and events that are most recent or that loom largest in your life, but as the minutes pass, you may find that some of the people and events that come to mind later and more gradually are the ones that surprise and touch you most deeply.

Consider what love has looked and felt like at various times in your life. What do these memories tell you about how God's love might feel? What do they suggest about how you might express love for God and neighbour?

———————

Sketch, colour, sculpt or paint an image of your relationship with God. Relationships can be complicated and multi-faceted, so feel free to create one or many images. Does one of your images correspond to the relationship you most desire with God? If not, sketch that relationship. If what you originally sketched conformed to your ideal, try sketching a way or ways that you sometimes relate to God that do not conform to that ideal. Now consider what might stand in the way – sometimes or most of the time or all the time – of the relationship you'd wish to have. Could any dimension of the love commandment enrich your image of your relationship with God? Does one of the dimensions best describe how you think of love? Does any suggest something new to you?

———•◦•———

Read aloud the story of the man Jesus loves (10.17–31). If you are in a group, perhaps have different people take the roles of Jesus, the man and the disciples.

Notice that the story is framed by references to Jesus' 'way' to Jerusalem (10.17, translated *journey*, NRSV; 10.32, *road*), and so the invitation to follow is an invitation to take that way with Jesus. Remember also that the demands Jesus places are out of love and that in giving things up in order to follow Jesus, the disciples have found the very key to eternal life that the man seeks (10.17, 30).

After your reading, reflect on what Jesus might ask you to give up because he loves you. Might anything be limiting your capacity to follow Jesus wholeheartedly on the way of love? Are there things you feel you would like to give up with the assurance that 'for God all things are possible' (10.27)?

Imagine Jesus telling you he loves you. Imagine him as vividly as you can. What does he look like? How old is he? Where are the two of you? Now imagine him inviting you to let go of those things that limit, to exchange them for heavenly treasure and follow him. What might you say to him, or how might you react now, given that he does in fact love you and you are actually even now and every day invited to follow him?

———•◦•———

Read Philippians 3.7–14 in which Paul talks about how he came to regard his excellent CV as rubbish in light of Christ's presence in his life.

In your mind, scan your past for things that you see as particular successes or failures, or things that would count as such on a normal

CV. Put those aside for now along with anything that you imagine you could not carry with you into the kingdom of God. God's kingdom doesn't take money; we can't lug a house or a car through the gate; the natural beauty of the lilies is high fashion (Luke 12.22–34).

When you shed the armour of your CV and set aside your past successes and failures, how do you feel? Does this help you see more clearly what God sees in you and how God might wish to make you blossom in love? Where do you already see love (God's and yours) bearing fruit in your life? As you think about how you, like Paul, might forget what lies behind and press on towards the future on God's more excellent way, read Galatians 5.22–23 and Ephesians 6.10–17, and see if anything there might strengthen your heavenly CV.

Read/perform Mark 12. If you are in a group, present the sections of the chapter to one another in sub-groups; if you are only two sub-groups, take alternate sections as you move through the chapter. As you assign roles, consider including the characters in the parable of the vineyard and the Sadducees' tale; the scribes in 12.38–40; the widow and the wealthy at the temple treasury. As there would be so many roles to play, you might ask for volunteers from your audience to participate.

As you perform and experience the performances of others, think about what Jesus' teachings in this chapter suggest about living life with love as the source and goal of all things. Perhaps make notes as you go along and then have a time of discussion at the end.

7

Following the King

———•◆•———

Focus text	Mark 15.33–39
Reading through Mark	Mark 14—15
Poetry to pray	Psalm 22
Supplementary passages	Amos 8.9–10
	Isaiah 52.13—53.12
	John 13.36—14.4
	Romans 8.14–17, 31–39
	Revelation 5.1–14
Words to take with you	Truly this man was God's Son!

———•◆•———

THINKING ABOUT MARK 15.33–39

The coronation of the king

Finally we come to the terrible death of the Son, betrayed, denied and deserted by his male followers; mocked by passers-by, who shake their heads and say 'Aha', and by the religious authorities, who have condemned him in a kangaroo court and handed him over to the Romans for a barbaric death; even the ones crucified with him find the strength to join in the taunts.

At noon, darkness covers the whole land in what might be a mini-dissolution of the cosmos, evoking that suffering beyond all suffering that Jesus has spent much of Mark 13 describing. That prediction of suffering to come has created a suitable backdrop for the passion, which stretches over two chapters, thick with irony and laden with beatings and bindings and abuse and then the naked agony of the cross. At three o'clock in the afternoon, Jesus borrows the words of a psalm of lament to express the depths beyond which he can sink no further, his abandonment by the one who has torn through the heavens to declare love and pleasure in him, the Abba Father to whom he has made his final heart-rending prayers in a state of agitation and distress at Gethsemane.

Then at last someone on earth other than the unclean spirits sees who he is in himself, independent of what he can do for anyone in their personal chaos, independent of his charismatic preaching and powerful hem. As he cries his final great cry and breathes his last, one of his executioners sees and hears and says: 'Truly this man was God's Son!'

There is a sense in which this ending brings us back full circle to the prologue (1.1–15), but with everything turned upside down and inside out. Where Jesus was identified there by the voice of parental love descending on him with the Spirit-dove, here it is a Roman soldier who recognizes the holy Son as he dies on a cross. Where there the voice crying in the wilderness was the prophetic voice of John the Baptist embodying Isaiah's hopeful words of restoration, here the voice crying out is Jesus' own from the wilderness of the cross.[1] Where there the heavens were torn apart as Jesus rose from the Jordan in the rebirth of baptism, here it is the temple curtain that tears as he dies, signalling not the boundlessness of love but divine judgement of an institution that has become love's opposite.

It is a kind of undoing but also clearly a completion of the battle between Jesus and Satan that began in that wilderness, and it marks the arrival of the kingdom that Jesus proclaimed immediately after those 40 days and 40 nights. In a way that no one could have predicted, God's Anointed One has ascended to his throne. The inscription of the charge against him on the cross finally says who he is for all the world to see: King. Rome's own army has adorned him in purple and crowned him with thorns before stripping him and lifting him up, and now it is one of their officers who stands beneath him and affirms what the heavenly voice said from above.

And if the tearing of the curtain points to destruction, it also indicates again that God will not be contained. The one whose absence

Jesus laments has in the very moment of seeming defeat ripped through to earth with his life-giving reign.

The lament of the king

Mark's account of the suffering and death of Jesus is dark and disorientating. In that way it has much in common with the psalms of lament, also called psalms of darkness or disorientation. In addition to echoing specific psalms of lament, the whole of the passion is something like a psalm of lament being played out before our eyes. Jesus himself draws on one of these when he uses the words of Psalm 22.1 in his cry from the cross. The narrator evokes Psalm 22.18 in the reference to the division of Jesus' garments and the casting of lots. The threefold mocking by passers-by (the verb in 15.29 is the basis for the word *blasphemy*), religious authorities and even the bandits crucified with Jesus also echoes the lament of that Psalmist (22.7–8): 'All who see me mock at me; they make mouths at me, they shake their heads: "Commit your cause to the LORD; let him deliver – let him rescue the one in whom he delights!"'

Mark highlights Jesus' suffering more than any other Gospel. Particularly because the account of the resurrection in Mark is so brief (eight verses, versus 56 in John, 53 in Luke and 20 in Matthew), the passion looms large. This is especially clear in comparison with John.

In John the arresting party falls to the ground at Jesus' 'I am' and has to be directed by Jesus to arrest him. The references to torture aside from the crucifixion itself are one blow by one of the temple police, whom Jesus rebukes, and two and a half verses in which Pilate has Jesus flogged and the soldiers robe him in purple, crown him with thorns, strike him and hail him as King of the Jews. In Mark, by contrast, even before he is handed over to Pilate, Jesus is blindfolded, spat upon and beaten by the religious authorities and their guards. The account of his torture by the Roman cohort is more than twice as long as John's and includes his being stripped of the purple robe, something that is mentioned only later in John (prisoners were normally crucified naked), such that he is still wearing the robe and crown in John 19.5 as Pilate displays him to the crowd and says, 'Behold the man!' (KJV).

On the cross in John 19.26–30 Jesus, attended by people who love him, speaks with his mother and the disciple whom he loves and, in fulfilment of Scripture, says he is thirsty and is given a sponge full of wine on a branch of hyssop, a detail evoking the sacrifice of the Passover lamb. At the appropriate time, he announces that all is completed and gives up his spirit with so much intentionality that some see it as a giving of the Holy Spirit. In Mark, as he is being crucified, Jesus is offered wine mixed with myrrh, a painkiller and, therefore, a reminder of the brutality of this form of execution. Then, surrounded by strangers and enemies, he is mocked by every possible group. When he cries out with a loud voice, echoing the desperate cries of demoniacs earlier in Mark,[2] his words of lament are misunderstood by the strangers around him, who offer him a sponge full of wine on a stick, which in this context could be another act of derision, in response to what they think is a hopeless call for Elijah. Finally, after another great cry, he breathes his last.

Mark's passion emphasizes the extended agony, helplessness and isolation of Jesus.

Mark among the Gospels focuses most on suffering throughout his narrative, not only in the passion. We see this in the central section (8.22—10.52) with Jesus' threefold prediction of the passion-resurrection and his teaching on what this will mean for his followers. We see it in the pre-passion Jerusalem chapters (Mark 11—13), where the conflict with Jesus' opponents intensifies and the inevitability of Jesus' suffering and death becomes increasingly clear; and Jesus also makes very clear that his followers will face the same violent resistance. From the beginning, even before Jesus' first reference to his execution, there are hints of what is to come: in the reference to John's arrest immediately before Jesus begins to preach (1.14) and in the account of John's death (6.17–29); in Jesus' reference to the loss of the bridegroom (2.20); and in the determination of the Pharisees and the Herodians to destroy him (3.6).

We also observed in our study of Jesus as healer in Mark 5 that Mark's account lingers long enough for us to see the suffering that brings each of the people to this point in their stories; and then it does not rush to resolution but gives us glimpses of the new life that follows Jesus' acts of restoration. We saw rhetoric of passion and resurrection sprinkled throughout those accounts: tombs and stones, body and blood, dying and rising, all pointing us forward to Mark's larger story of the dying and rising Christ.

Their stories offer faint echoes of his larger story, and in some ways he is just like them and us. But in addition to being one of us, he is also God-with-us. When he cries out to the Father in his particularity as God's beloved Son, he carries in himself all the laments of the world, and he is also in himself God's answer.

Asking God why

Jesus accepts God's will in the cross but not without asking that it be removed (14.36) and not without a final cry of forsakenness. That cry, Jesus' last words in Mark, is not only a lament; it is a rebuke in the form of a question: Why?

That this lament is taken from a psalm places it in the context of faithfulness, not only Jesus' own faithfulness but also the faithfulness of Israel as it is expressed in Psalm 22 and in the whole of the Psalter. We also in the context of our lives of faith should be able to find room to lay before God all of ourselves and our experiences of the world. We can do this hand in hand with Jesus and can, if we wish, borrow faithful words of sorrow, rage, isolation and rebuke from the Psalmists.

Suffering is not an aberration in the life of the believer any more than it is in any human life. Life, though beautiful, is also difficult, sometimes particularly so and in ways we do not anticipate. We sometimes imply in churches that if we do faith right and are close to Jesus, this will be demonstrated in our lives by a lack of suffering and sorrow or by a uniformly peaceful acceptance of them. But if we look at Jesus himself and at others of God's chosen ones in Scripture, this turns out to be a great, and sometimes destructive, distortion.

Scripture also makes clear to us that it is completely appropriate to acknowledge that we are suffering. Not only that, we are invited to say this openly to God, to speak to God from our depths as we speak from our heights. Jesus draws on the biblical tradition of open, honest lament in his moment of greatest agony. By drawing on this tradition ourselves, we find that we can bring all that we are to God and that we then experience all of life as part of our life of faith. If we do not do this, then when things go desperately wrong or when we are angry or doubting or God seems far away, we may be more likely to feel that we have travelled outside the bounds of God's love or that we have left the territory of faith and wandered into a wilderness alone. In fact, the wilderness is part of the story of faith. It is all part of it.

When we see suffering as part of life, and therefore as part of our life as people of faith, we can also see beyond it into God's eternal love, which sustains us even when we do not feel it and moves us towards God's future even when we can see nothing but absence and death and an end.

Friends of the king

As Scripture invites us to bring all of ourselves to God, it also teaches us to accept that when we do this, we will inevitably find that God gets our best and our worst. We are complicated, and the people around us are complicated. That is perhaps why Jesus and the evangelists and other writers of our sacred texts make things as simple as possible by summing it all up with the command to love God and neighbour. If we start there and keep returning to that aim when we have strayed, knowing that God is always calling us back with his gracious love that precedes our love, then we'll be on the right track.

God seeks and calls human beings to be bearers of light and love in the world, earthen vessels for holy treasure. Then Jesus, God's Beloved in whom God's soul delights, also opts not to go through life in glorious isolation. He asks people to follow him, and he responds to people who gravitate to him for any reason.

Even at the end, in the final chapters of his life and Mark's story, although Jesus knows that people who have followed him will fail him, betray him and desert him, he keeps inviting them into his life and assures them that he will be part of their future. And even at this stage in his story, at the very point when he is also, in a sense, most alone, there are new characters around him, doing what they can (14.8).

As we consider the characters who in some way serve as friends to Jesus in Mark 14—15, or try to and fail, we find that their interactions with Jesus, while always telling us something about him, also offer us places in which we might locate ourselves in the story and come, or return, to him with our own love, faithfulness, failings and fears.

The anointing

The passion account begins with the determination of the religious authorities to arrest Jesus by stealth and kill him. Their plotting and Judas' participation in their plans frame the account of Jesus' anointing and lend urgency and poignancy to it (14.1–2, 10–11).

The anointing (14.3–9) is hosted by a leper and performed by a woman, making it a fitting tribute for a boundary-crossing saviour, whom the scribes – who are among the plotters of 14.1 – have condemned for his unsuitable dinner partners. The woman is unnamed and audacious (and is, in those respects, similar to the anonymous woman of Luke 7.36–50; the anointer in John 12.1–8 is Mary of Bethany; the association of the anointing with Mary Magdalene has no biblical basis and emerged centuries later). She interrupts the dinner party to anoint Jesus' head with an expensive aromatic oil. In an act worthy of the one who loves God and neighbour with radical abundance, as Jesus always does, his anointer transforms a normal act into an act of gracious, extravagant beauty. Not only is the oil expensive (worth about a year's wages); she also uses all of it, even breaking the jar so that every drop pours over him and even the jar itself is offered in the act.

Her gift is met with protest. It is wasteful, they say. And some of us may find at one time or another that our most heartfelt gifts to God are misunderstood and may even appear to be a waste of our talents or our time in the eyes of those who cannot see our hearts as Jesus can, and sometimes it is impossible to explain even to those closest to us. But Jesus does recognize her act of love, that she has done what she could for him, which is all that is asked of us, and she has done it completely. It isn't that the poor are less important; the verse Jesus borrows from Deuteronomy 15.11 goes on to speak of care for the poor, and Jesus himself speaks of it in Mark 10.21. It is that hers is a differently beautiful gift, right for this moment in God's plans for the kingdom.

Jesus identifies this as an anointing for death. There is evidence that jars of oil used for anointing corpses were left broken at the tomb. So her broken, empty jar points both to her love poured out and his body broken in death.

While it is part of the story of his death, her act also begins the story of his coronation, his lifting up as king. *Messiah* and *Christ* mean anointed; this anointing would normally be by priests, who were always men.[3] But in the beautifully upside-down kingdom of God, a woman can be remembered, wherever the story is told, as the one who anointed the eternal king.

The last night

Mark's account of Jesus' last night and the preparation for it (14.12–72), like the account of the anointing, is also a story of the people around him, and in this case they are his closest companions. While some new characters introduced in the passion act as friends of the Messiah, some in extravagant ways, the ones from whom faithfulness would be most anticipated fail him. But because we know – as even Mark's earliest audiences knew – what these people later became, we can also see in them ways in which our own failings may not be an end but may instead lead us back into the arms of grace and on into new life.

Jesus knows that they will all leave him, that one will betray him, that the most vocally ardent among them will deny him. But he also knows that this will not be an ending. So he continues trying to prepare them for both, as he has all along: He calls them towards the future he knows waits for them even as he prepares them for imminent failure and despair.

The preparations for the Passover begin mysteriously (14.12–16), but this is not unusual with Jesus. Two disciples are sent into the city with a message for a man with a jug as two disciples earlier went off in search of a donkey with a message to any who questioned them (11.1–10). Here they are led to the upper room of the Last Supper that they do not know will be the last.

As they are eating (14.17–25), Jesus tells them the bitter news that one of them will betray him, and they enter into a fog of confusion that will hang over them for the rest of their story in Mark 14. Their confusion is so deep that they do not insist adamantly that they will not betray him but instead ask for confirmation, one by one: 'Surely not I?'

Then Jesus tells them the words that they will remember and repeat: 'Take; this is my body.' And they eat and take his presence into their frail flesh. Then he offers them the cup, and they drink in the good news of his new covenant. They do not understand what it means, and they do not have to understand, any more than we do. They have him, and that is the point, for them and for us. Then he points them towards the newness of the kingdom so that his death, his promise that he will 'never again drink', seems to foretell a triumphal entry rather than a defeat. The meal points towards death and towards greater life, for them and for us. And after the meal they sing a hymn, as we do.

Then they go out to the Mount of Olives (14.26–42) where he tells them that they will scatter like sheep when he is struck down. Peter, who has spoken in ardent haste before, does so again, and now all of them follow him in insisting that rather than deny Jesus, they will die for him. They insist that they will be able to take the way of discipleship of 8.34.

But, of course, they cannot. Even the three who have seen him raise a dead little girl, witnessed his radiance on the mountaintop and heard the voice of divine love claiming him cannot manage to be present for Jesus in his dark night of the soul.

Then it is all over for them. He is arrested, and they scatter. All except two.

The young man in the linen cloth lingers longer than most (14.51–52). The word for *linen cloth* is the same word used for Jesus' burial shroud (15.46). The young man is, it seems, dressed for death, but when it grabs hold of him, he leaves his shroud behind and flees naked.

Then there is Peter (14.54, 66–72). His story, interwoven with the account of Jesus' interrogation before the Sanhedrin, is the beginning of every story of every person who follows Jesus into danger. Most of us will not face the threat of death, but even with the threat of loss of some part of ourselves, not our very *psyche* (the soul/life of 8.35–37; 12.30) but something that we believe to be central to our identity, it can become difficult not to deny him. We may all of us at one time – or many times – fail to hold fast. Like seeds among thorns, we may be lured by wealth, choked by the cares of the world or distracted by desires for other things.

But in the moments when we come to ourselves and weep at the extent to which we have lost our way, we might remember the rest of Jesus' words to his own that night. When the cock crows and Peter remembers Jesus telling him that he would deny him (14.30) and telling all of them that they would scatter and fall away (14.27), Peter does not remember the good news, nestled between the two predictions of failure (14.28): the assurance that this story is not over.

The death

For now, at least, Jesus' closest male companions are gone. But two new characters are drawn into Jesus' story.

Simon of Cyrene is pressed into service on the way to Golgotha (15.21). The implication is that Jesus is too weak to carry his own cross because of the extent of the earlier abuse. *Simon* is a Jewish name, so he is a diaspora Jew from North Africa, the father of two people whose names seem meant to ring a bell: 'You know Alexander and Rufus,' Mark appears to be saying. 'It was their dad who carried his cross.' And so another Simon, not the one we left weeping in the high priest's courtyard, becomes the first to take up the cross and follow.

Then, after the death, it is a member of the Sanhedrin who dares to go to Pilate, to identify himself with an enemy of the state and to risk being viewed as one himself (15.42–46). Jesus' disciples have deserted him, but this Joseph comes forward from a most unlikely quarter, bringing with him his hopes for the kingdom of God. And so at this moment when Jesus has died, our minds are drawn back full circle to the beginning when we heard Jesus' invitation to believe the good news that the time was fulfilled and the kingdom of God was at hand. The Son has drunk the cup and been baptized with the baptism with which he had to be baptized (10.38; 14.36). As Joseph of Arimathea holds the body of Jesus, his hopes are fulfilled. The kingdom of God is in his arms.

The waiting

After Jesus breathes his last we meet another group of followers. We've not heard of them before, but they were always there, and it all ends with them looking on, first at the cross, then at the tomb (15.40–41, 47). They have followed him from his beginnings in Galilee, as we have, and now they will lead us into the final chapter. But first there is the long silence of Saturday that hangs over the chapter break as the world within the text pauses at the tomb, and we pause and pray and mourn with it.

SUGGESTIONS FOR PRAYER AND EMBODIMENT

Choose a character from Mark 14—15 who draws you: the anointing woman; the disciples – sent to prepare the Passover, at the Last Supper or on the Mount of Olives; the young man who runs away; the centurion; Joseph of Arimathea. Pray the passage(s) about that character; let it stay with you for a day or two if you wish.

Consider why this character at this moment in the narrative draws you. In what ways might this story or character connect with your life, your hopes, your fears? Express your connection or interest in the character with dance, writing, paint, crayon, construction paper, magazine clippings, clay or objects you have on hand in your house or garden, or in some other way.

If you are in a group, you may wish to leave time for those who would like to do so to speak about the character they chose. You could speak as the character remembering that moment or as another character remembering what that character did; for example, you might present the anointing woman from the perspective of Simon the leper. Or you could share something you created and perhaps speak about what drew you to this character.

Reread the anointing (14.3–9); you might have a pleasing fragrance in the room as you read (fresh lavender; incense; orange and cloves boiling on the stove).

Think about times when you have given a gift, especially something that surprised or moved you or the recipient; it could be something helpful or thoughtful you did. Jot down those moments as you remember them. What moved you to do those things? What did they feel like?

Now remember times when you have been surprised by the thoughtfulness, kindness or sheer unexpectedness of something someone did for you or gave to you. It could be something small, an affirmation from a friend or something a stranger did for you in the street. Or it could be something big, something above and beyond the call of duty. Jot these down too.

As you look at your lists, what strikes you? Do you notice anything about what has made you happiest or most touched you? Is there anything that surprises you?

Is there something you might wish to do for someone now? Something you might wish to do for Jesus? There is a lovely film called *Babette's Feast*, based on an equally lovely story by Isak Dinesen, about an extravagant and beautiful gift, which you might view or read as inspiration.[4] You might also read Matthew 25.34–40.

———————

Read aloud 14.12–36. If you are in a group, ask people to read Jesus' words in turn: the first will read Jesus' words in 14.13–15, the second his words in 14.18, the third 14.20–21, the fourth 14.22 and so on. In 14.19, have everyone join in saying the words, 'Surely not I?' After 14.25, pause to sing a hymn appropriate for your group. (In the UK a good possibility is 'My song is love unknown'; in the USA, 'What wondrous love is this'.) At the end of the reading, after 14.36, pause for meditation on Jesus' prayer, to pray his words as your own or to listen for God, remembering that we are also God's children invited to pray to him as our Abba Father (Romans 8.14–17; Galatians 4.6).

———————

Think of a time when you felt you let down someone you loved. Maybe you believe that you have let God down at some point. If there is a time that still troubles you, reflect on that time, in particular. With that in mind, read aloud the story of Peter's threefold denial (14.66–72), either alone or in your group. When he breaks down and weeps as he realizes what he has done, pause to consider the thing you regret. Offer that thing to God and lay before him your regret.

Now go back to 14.26–31 and notice that after Jesus tells his disciples that they will desert him, he reassures them that he will see them again in Galilee. You might wish also to read John 13.36—14.7, in which Jesus' insistence that Peter will not be able to follow him at that time but will follow later is preceded by the commandment to love one another and immediately followed by some of the most comforting words in all of Scripture. Sit with either Mark 14.28 or John 14.1, and hear Jesus say those words to you. Then hear him telling you that nothing in your past will keep you from following God's good way for you now and in the future.

———•◆•———

In reading 15.33–39 on your own or with your group, consider pausing after 15.34 to read the whole of Psalm 22 from which Jesus draws his lament. You might wish to pray it as your own prayer. As Jesus borrows the words of the Psalmist, so we also are invited to pray the Psalms, as some religious orders do on a daily basis. If you cannot relate to the words of Psalm 22 now, was there another time when you could? If not, who among your acquaintances or in another part of the world might be able to relate to the words? Pray the words for yourself or someone else. Then return to 15.35–39.

If you are presenting the text to a group, consider also having fabric to tear when the curtain of the temple is torn from top to bottom. Suggest to the group in advance that as they hear the tearing of the curtain, they might also remember the tearing of the heavens and imagine God's love pouring through it over all of you like light and the Spirit descending like a dove and resting in the middle of the room. Pause for a moment for people to experience the love and the Spirit. Then begin again with the final verse, and invite everyone to say together the centurion's words: 'Truly this man was God's Son!'

8

Into the Silence

---◆◆◆---

Focus text	Mark 16.1–8
Poetry to pray	Song of Songs 2.10–13, 16–17
Supplementary passages	Matthew 28.16–20 Luke 24.13–35 John 20.1–18 John 21.15–19 Philippians 2.1–13
Words to take with you	There you will see him, just as he told you.

---◆◆◆---

THINKING ABOUT MARK 16.1–8

The women

They have been in the story all along, but silent and invisible, unnamed like the woman with her alabaster jar, until now. Even once some of them are named, at the death and the burial (15.40–41, 47), still they are motionless and voiceless. They cannot even be said to be witnesses since their testimony to the events would not be legally meaningful in the world of this tale. So, like us, they can only be said to watch from a distance and to move only as they are conveyed along by events in which they play no part.

Until suddenly, in 16.1, they spring into action, continuing the process that was paused for the deathly silence of this Sabbath, and we see them doing what they were invisibly doing all along, all the way from his beginning in Galilee, ministering to him like his angels in the wilderness. In Mark, the Greek word for *ministering* (or *serving*) is used only of women (1.31; 15.41), of angels (1.13) and of the Son (10.45). And now we see them at it. Once the Sabbath ends on Saturday evening, they buy their aromatic oils, no pure nard as far as we know, but the proper things of death.

Then early in the morning, encircled in light, they are in motion again, and they have voices. They are reviewing the scenery of 15.46 – the tomb and the stone – and the stone is a problem. These door-keepers who have kept watch faithfully through it all (13.34) do not now have entry to the absent master's house. But still they go. And they find that the master has prepared the way, or someone has. The door is open. Someone is at home.

Then more disorientation (the word for their reaction in 16.5–6 describes Jesus' distress at Gethsemane, 14.33), because it is not the master, living or dead, but an intruder in the white robe of holiness and martyrdom, of baptism and rebirth, of angels and awe. He tells them not to feel what they feel, but we all know that never works because feelings are like rain, and theirs were surely already torrential before the Sabbath in the grief-flood of his death.

Then this young man tells them some of what they already know. He proclaims to them the absence: he is not here. He refers to Jesus' origins in Nazareth, which they know well, they who followed him from Galilee (perhaps some of them have known him for years, saw him grow up, grow different and wondrous). He speaks the perfect participle that extends from the cross into for ever: that Jesus has become and will for ever remain the one who has been crucified.

But in the midst of all of this is something they do not already know, something even more disorientating than his absence: he has been raised.

Before they can process this or remember that Jesus always said that life would follow death, the intruder sends them away, clutching their spices of death. He makes these ministering, following, watching women into messengers, which in Greek would be *angeloi*, angels. Or, put another way, they are sent ones, which in Greek would be *apostoloi*, apostles. They are sent like apostles to tell like angels the terrible, beautiful news that the one who is still called crucified – because that can never be undone – is now for ever something else. They are to go to the scattered flock and their courageous, temporarily tragic spokesman and tell them that Jesus is going before them to Galilee, back to the place of their beginnings. But this is not a call to rewind and start anew. The perfect tense of the crucifixion and the emptiness of the tomb ensure that there is no starting over again; there is only moving on. The one who came home to Galilee from the Jordan and the wilderness all those chapters ago is for ever changed – for ever scarred and for ever glorious. And so everything will change for them now too.

Beyond words

Our earliest accounts of the resurrection come from Paul's letters; there we hear of Jesus' appearances (1 Corinthians 15.3–11). Then the other Gospel writers also tell of these encounters, and they add that the first were with women, which Paul doesn't mention, but that may be because they would not be considered compelling witnesses, so why bother?

Our expectations have been shaped by those other accounts, which all tend to conflate in our minds, just as all of the beginnings conflate until finally we have an image of a star over a manger and magi nestled next to shepherds on the mantelpiece, which isn't faithful to any particular Gospel but is a lovely blending of two. Similarly our several resurrection accounts meld into one, and so when we say 'resurrection', we hear the Great Commission (Matthew 28.18–20); we see Mary Magdalene weeping, then turning as the gardener-Jesus calls her name (John 20.11–18); we find ourselves on the dusty road to Emmaus, then sitting at table with Jesus as he breaks the bread and scales fall from our eyes (Luke 24.13–35); then we are standing on the shore of the Sea of Galilee, and there he is with an abundance of freshly caught fish, offering us breakfast, and we hear him ask again and again, 'Do you love me?' and ourselves saying again and again, 'Yes, you know that I love you', and his response, over and over: 'Feed my sheep' (John 21.1–19).

When we come to a single Gospel, we know we will not hear all of it, but we expect every Gospel ending to evoke all the others in some way.

Mark does not meet those expectations.

If Mark ended at 16.7, we might be happy enough all the same, we and all of the readers and hearers of the Gospels stretching across the centuries before us. But, of course, it does not end there. Having nearly tied up the loose ends of the story, Mark unties them again in 16.8: 'So they went out and fled from the tomb, for terror and amazement had seized them; and they said nothing to anyone, for they were afraid.'

In an essay on Gospel endings, William Placher writes, 'the Gospels' ends shock us into the story.'[1] He says this of all of them, but it seems particularly true of John, where we get a surfeit of endings, and Mark, where something seems to be missing. It is not only we who feel it. It was true from the earliest centuries when people added what we now call the shorter ending, 16.8b, and the longer ending, 16.9–20. There is no doubt that these were added later. It is now accepted in academic circles that Mark as we know it ends at 16.8 and, furthermore, that there need not have been more. But we do not have any consensus about what we are to make of this.

Some try to interpret the unsettledness out of the text. This is possible if we go back to 16.7 and dwell in the promise of the young man. We are justified in doing this because he is only repeating what Jesus already predicted many times and then, in 14.28, assured his followers would happen: that he would be raised and would go before them to Galilee. The audience of Mark has always known in advance that the story would end with a risen Lord. Whether the women tell it or they don't, Jesus has been raised; Peter and the others will see him again; the church will be set alight by the power of the Holy Spirit; the word will advance.

But that is not where Mark ends his story, and so to dwell there rejoicing at the empty tomb while the women run away is fine, but it is not faithful to this particular account of God's best news.

Another way to understand the ending is to say that the fear the women experience is awe, and this is also perfectly possible. The same Greek word describes both kinds of fear – holy awe and unholy terror. And who wouldn't feel a sense of awe at the realization that someone whom they saw die a terrible death and whom they love deeply has been raised?

Their trembling (the literal meaning of the word translated *terror* in the NRSV) and amazement are also understandable. Who would not tremble at such an experience, and feel amazed? This word for amazement is *ecstasis*, from which we get our word *ecstasy*; we have seen it before in the witnesses to the raising of the little girl (5.42). Trembling and a trance-like state of awe sound right for a resurrection, certainly more appropriate for an adult Easter than chocolate bunnies. Even the women's flight might, at a stretch, be interpreted in a positive light, although everyone else who flees in the Gospel is fleeing from Jesus or from destruction (5.14; 14.50–52; 13.14). But after all, Jesus is not there, and they have been told to go, and they go.

The problem with this interpretation is that it falls apart at the end when we learn that they tell nothing to anyone. It is one of Mark's emphatic double negatives: they tell no one nothing.

That is where the story ends. Beyond words.

And so if we want to be as faithful as possible to this narrative's particular rendition of God's good news and to stick with it to the very end, that is where we find ourselves – with women who, for now and for as long as we choose to stay alongside them and this story, are not ready to speak.

Perhaps they do feel awe and their terror is temporary. Maybe it is that their story isn't quite finished. Maybe, like the woman in the crowd at 5.29, they feel the power of life surging around them, but it is still cloaked in fear and will stay that way until they run all the way into the arms of Jesus, and he lifts them back into full voice. Maybe he will find them as soon as they leave the frame of the narrative. Maybe he is waiting on the very next page of their lives.

But that page is not part of our good news. We are given this page. This page with no more words.

And perhaps the silence is a strange gift.

Perhaps it isn't always possible in the space of a chapter break, the breath between two verses, to move from the horror of the cross and the heaviness of the precious linen-shrouded corpse straight out into eternal light. Perhaps we, like the women, need some time to sit or run in silence and take in the enormity of it all, to let the sound of the lament of the dying Son settle for a bit longer before we rejoice at the good news of the empty tomb.

Maybe it is a good thing to run alongside them in their silence and see them tremble and take in some of their *ecstasis* and their awe-full terror.

It is certainly possible to speak of failure here. The young man says, 'Tell'; and they say nothing. But even he may be read alongside the only other young man of this Gospel (14.51–52), the one who sheds his linen shroud of death and runs for his life as Jesus is taken away to the cross. Perhaps we have twin images even here of the fellow who tried to follow and failed and then his white-robed redemption in this figure who tells God's best news when it matters most. Maybe he gives us hope for these ministering women who flee now.

But since we don't have the other pages of their lives, who are we to judge anyway. And the same could be said of each of us. With God, there are always more pages to come. Life is never settled. When we see what looks like disaster, confusion and a lost cause in ourselves or others, it is always provisional. For God, all things are possible. If an empty tomb is possible, all things are always possible in God's eternal 'already' and 'not quite yet'.

So we are invited to run straight into the mystery and the silence and to discover what our own next pages will say, what impossible possible new thing he will do in us next, and what impossible possible thing he will call us to do with him.

SUGGESTIONS FOR PRAYER AND EMBODIMENT

Create an image to express your experience of Mark's ending. This could be something personal to you or an image from the story, whatever strikes you (you don't have to know why): the spices; the early morning light; the massive stone rolled away from the door; the white robe of the young man; his words; the women's silent flight. If nothing comes to mind, pray the passage and see what lingers in your mind or causes you to stop and think. If you are in a group, consider having clay or modelling dough for this gathering. If those are accessible to you on your own, you could do that at home. Or you might use objects from your garden to create something.

As you look at what you have created, what does your reaction to the ending tell you about yourself? Does it suggest anything about God or Jesus in the Gospel of Mark or in your life?

Imagine going to the tomb with two people you know. Who comes to mind? How would each of you react to the prospect of anointing Jesus, to the realization that there is no one to roll away the stone, to the sight of the young man and the absence of the body, to the proclamation and instruction? Now reread Mark's account of the crucifixion and burial of Jesus, and imagine yourself and your two friends witnessing those events. Does that change how you imagine yourself reacting at the tomb?

Think of times when you have been silenced, at a loss for words, or had your breath knocked out of you by something you saw or experienced. Make a list if you wish. If you are rarely left speechless, you might think of times when your fight-or-flight mechanism kicked in (trembling hands and pounding heart). Sit with these experiences for a little while. What were the feelings that came with your silence or your fight-or-flight moments? Were the things all hard things? Were some intensely happy or beautiful? Do these memories give you any new insights into the silent flight of the women?

In the presentation of 16.1–8, or at some point in your personal contemplation of it, consider beginning with 15.33–47. Then have a time of silence for the experience of Saturday between 15.47 and 16.1; try to have at least three minutes, but you can determine this based on how you or your group handles silence. In the silence, consider the experience of the women at the crucifixion and the experience

97

of helplessness on the Saturday. If you have lost someone you love, you might remember how you felt in the immediate aftermath. If you or someone you love has experienced violence, that experience might also help you understand the experience of these women, but be gentle with yourself and do not go to any place that is too painful for you. Feel free to remain in the moment with the text if that is better for you.

After the silence, continue with the presentation of 16.1–8. At the end, as the women flee, have another time of silence; again try to have at least three minutes. Flee with these women in your mind's eye. You might imagine yourself as one of them, or you might go alongside them. Consider where they (you) might go. Imagine the feeling of the earth under your feet, the feeling of your heart pumping, your breathing quickening, all of the physical sensations of fear and flight. Are they/you still holding the spices that you have bought the evening before and taken to the tomb for his body? Imagine carrying those or watching someone else carry them. In your own time, allow the news to sink in that Jesus is waiting for you.

Now bring yourself fully into the present moment. Notice the sensations in your body, the feel of the air in the room, your weight against the chair and the floor, any sounds, any smells. Relax any parts of yourself that may have become tense in this experience (your shoulders; your face) and sit up comfortably. Take a deep breath.

Now again allow the news to sink in: Jesus is waiting for you.

Epilogue: Embodying Mark

Focus text   The Gospel of Mark

Words to take with you   Follow me.

The Gospel of Mark offers us the possibility of a future that is not sorted, not contained, not resolved, and in doing that, it comes alongside people for whom that is the case, which at some time or another is each of us. In this way the Gospel is both wonderful and heart-rendingly realistic.

Mark does not present Jesus' followers as people whose lives are devoid of pain and struggle. On the contrary, the Gospel offers us plenty of examples of both, none more so than Jesus himself. Jesus enters into places of great pain, and his disciples go with him. But then they are also on hand to witness and to experience in themselves the breathtaking newness he brings as the kingdom of God comes near in him.

We are invited to bring to Jesus our broken, hungry, confused, sick, faithful, hopeful, fearful, longing, loving, seeking, unresolved selves. We are invited to offer all that we are, our light and beauty, our shadows and sorrows, and to watch him make more of our gifts than we could have imagined possible. We are invited to take the way of love that Jesus takes and to find our 'ownmost possibilities' there.[1]

We do this knowing that our journey to the heart of the good news, the heart of God, is always only just beginning. Even our familiarity with our own hearts is sometimes fleeting, and so it is not surprising that God's heart should remain a mystery. But taking the gospel journey to him helps us experience more and more the love that waits for us and that makes us blossom into the people we are created to be – faithful in spite of fear, generous in spite of our inherent tendency towards insecurity, believing in our unbelief, courageous in our confusion; willing to turn the page and try again when all seems lost because we know that all is never lost with him.

The bright and the holy in us may sometimes be less evident than the broken and the profane. When that happens, we can look to Peter and others who fall and come back. When we are silent, we can run with the speechless ministering women until we find the risen Lord and with him find our voices again, or for the first time.

Through it all, we are invited to live in the beautiful, mysterious borderlands of God, the in-between place where grace dwells, sheltered in the shadow of the cross, with the voice of divine love falling gently over us like spring rain, and with the radiance of the ever-crucified, ever-risen, ever-Beloved leading us on to a future of good news in which we will become more and more like him, ourselves the embodiment of love.

SUGGESTIONS FOR PRAYER AND EMBODIMENT

Reflect on your sojourn in the Gospel of Mark. In whatever way is right for you, express something about your experience as a whole – with words, paint, clay, dance or any other medium of expression.

As you consider Jesus as king, lover, beloved, shepherd, healer, teacher, and the very embodiment of the good news of the kingdom of God, do you find that any particular aspect of his person appeals to you most of all? Are their aspects that challenge you? Does this tell you anything interesting about yourself? Your past? Your future? What words or images might you use to describe Jesus now?

As you think back on what it means for people in the story to find and follow Jesus, does any of that resonate with your experience of him? Their journeys are marked by confusion, elation, need, desperation, faithfulness, longing, love, anguish, courage, fear, awe and ecstasy. What words or images might you use to describe your own journey?

———————•◦•———————

Read the Gospel of Mark aloud – alone, with your group or with a friend. If you are part of a congregation, you might wish to engage them in this. You could invite people to participate in the presentation, taking some of the parts (there are many possible parts!), or you could prepare it with only your own group members (or alone) and then invite others to your reading/performance.

Consider having a number of people read the role of Jesus. Try to enlist males and females of various ages, shapes, sizes, races, personality types and life experiences. Each person will reveal something different about Jesus' radiance, his humanity and his love.

Remind yourself of your experience with the Gospel along the way. If you wrote or sketched thoughts or saved other creative expressions, look at those again. Glance back through the 'Suggestions for prayer and embodiment' sections. If any of the exercises particularly struck you at the time, why do you suppose that was?

After you have heard the Gospel in full and reviewed your experience, consider one or all of these questions:

- How does your experience of the Gospel now differ from the experience you had before you began this exploration?
- What do you notice now that you didn't notice before?
- How might you embody the good news in your own life today or in days to come?

Notes

---

1 Into the Wilderness

1 The word for good news is *euangelion*, and so we call the Gospel writers *evangelists*, which means 'good-newsists'.

2 The word for *tempt* or *test* in 1.13 is used elsewhere only in 8.11, 10.2 and 12.15 of the Pharisees, who as soon as 3.6 will be seeking to destroy Jesus.

3 Following the Healer

1 As Joel Marcus puts it – *Mark 1—8: A New Translation with Introduction and Commentary*, Anchor Bible (New Haven, CT/London: Yale University Press, 2000), p. 342.

5 Following the Beloved

1 In Mark in the NRSV, the words *Messiah* and *Christ* (based on Hebrew and Greek words for *anointed*) are both translations of the same Greek word from which we get our word *Christ*. At the time of Jesus, the expectation was that this Anointed One would be a king, the ultimate heir of God's great anointed king David.

2 In a section entitled 'Maintaining the Tension' in his *Theology of the Old Testament* (Minneapolis, MN: Fortress Press, 1997, pp. 400–3), Walter Brueggemann discusses how the tension in the Old Testament between what he calls 'testimony' and 'countertestimony' is evident in the New Testament and in Christian tradition in the cross and resurrection of Jesus (p. 401, emphasis in original):

> Thus Friday is the day of countertestimony in the Christian tradition, centered in Jesus' recital of Psalm 22, but also including the taunts addressed to Jesus by those around the cross (Matt. 27.39–44). Clearly Easter is taken to be substantiation of the core testimony concerning Yahweh's faithful sovereignty and sovereign fidelity. There is a sense that Sunday resolved Friday, that the core testimony resolves the countertestimony – except that liturgically, *both claims linger*.

6 Following the Lover

1 The seventeenth-century mathematician and philosopher Blaise Pascal writes in his great theological work *Pensées* (*Thoughts*), 'Le coeur a ses raisons, que la raison ne connaît point' (Paris: Garnier Frères, 1958), p. 146, which means, 'The heart has its reasons, which reason does not know.'

7 Following the King

1 The Greek verb used in 15.34 appears elsewhere only at 1.3.
2 The Greek words describing Jesus' loud cries in 15.34, 37 appear elsewhere in Mark only at 1.26 and 5.7.
3 The Greek word for *anoint* in 14.8 is not the verb normally used for a royal anointing, but the scene evokes such a moment.
4 *Babette's Feast*, Denmark, 1987, direction and screenplay by Gabriel Axel, Artificial Eye. Based on the short story by Isak Dinesen (pen name of Karen Blixen), 'Babette's Feast', in her collection *Anecdotes of Destiny* (London: Michael Joseph, 1958; Penguin, 2006).

8 Into the Silence

1 William Placher, *Narratives of a Vulnerable God* (Louisville, KY: Westminster John Knox, 1994), p. 101.

Epilogue: Embodying Mark

1 Paul Ricoeur, *Figuring the Sacred*, ed. M. I. Wallace; trans. David Pellauer (Minneapolis, MN: Fortress Press, 1995), p. 232:

> The world of the text is what incites the reader, or the listener, to understand himself or herself in the face of the text and to develop, in imagination and sympathy, the self capable of inhabiting this world by deploying his or her ownmost possibilities there.

Scripture index

Scripture index

Scripture index